The British Army in Egypt 1801

An Underrated Army Comes of Age

Carole Divall

Helion & Company

Helion & Company Limited
Unit 8 Amherst Business Centre
Budbrooke Road
Warwick
CV34 5WE
England
Tel. 01926 499619
Fax 01217 114075
Email: info@helion.co.uk
Website: www.helion.co.uk
Twitter: @helionbooks
Visit our blog at http://blog.helion.co.uk/

Published by Helion & Company 2018
Designed and typeset by Mach 3 Solutions Ltd (www.mach3solutions.co.uk)
Cover designed by Paul Hewitt, Battlefield Design (www.battlefield-design.co.uk)
Printed by Henry Ling Limited, Dorchester

Text © Carole Divall 2018
Cover: 'Fragment of Egyptian architecture bearing medallions with portraits of the generals
commanding the British Army in Egypt and otherwise illustrative of the ever memorable conquest
of that country' (Philip James de Loutherbourg, 1806) (© Anne S.K. Brown Military Collection)

ISBN 978-1-911628-14-9

British Library Cataloguing-in-Publication Data.
A catalogue record for this book is available from the British Library.

For details of other military history titles published by Helion & Company Limited,
contact the above address, or visit our website: http://www.helion.co.uk

We always welcome receiving book proposals from prospective authors.

Contents

Introduction

I started working on this survey of the British Army in the final campaign of the French Revolutionary Wars soon after completing a study of Lieutenant General Sir Ralph Abercromby during the same wars. Consequently, it was inevitable that the spirit of that much loved and greatly lamented general would hover over what can only be described as his victorious achievement, carried out by his army, even after his death early in the campaign. For the men who finally ousted the French from Egypt, from generals like John Moore to the soldiers in the ranks, many of them new to the regular army, were his pupils.

My earliest encounter with Sir Ralph Abercromby occurred many years ago in the form of a picture. As a child I was given an illustrated history of Britain. Among the images that caught my attention was one of a wounded man – wounded and dying after a great victory, so the accompanying text suggested. This was not either of the familiar contemporary prints of the death of Abercromby. I suspect it was a later Victorian interpretation of the scene, heavy on pathos. I certainly had no idea who the wounded man might have been or even where Alexandria was. But there was something in his face, in his hand resting on a colleague's arm in a gesture of peaceful resignation, in the faces of those gathered around him, which appealed to my imagination. Young as I was, I realised there was something special about this man, and by implication something special about the battle he had won.

I did not meet Abercromby again until I was working on my first study of the 30th Foot, who were part of what I like to call the British Army of Egypt. This acquaintance was furthered in a later book because one of its subjects was also in the Army of Egypt. The more I familiarised myself with the events in Egypt in 1801, the more impressed I was with the man who set them in motion. At the same time I began to realise that here was a seminal British campaign. Both the man and the campaign were worthy of further examination, certainly; but so was the army that fought the campaign. A simple question would lie at the heart of such an examination. 'Why did this army achieve so much when previous campaigns had achieved so little?'

That is the question I have tried to answer in the present study.

I am not an author who likes to work in isolation, and once again I have to thank the many friends who have discussed the Egypt campaign with me, listened and advised. Particular thanks are due to Michael Crumplin FRCS who has offered so much information on the medical services, particularly the problems connected with ophthalmia and the other diseases endemic in Egypt. Lieutenant Colonel Downham, like me a great admirer of General Abercromby, has been most generous in making available unpublished material relevant to the campaign. Finally, I owe particular thanks to Andrew Bamford, friend and editor, who has consistently offered the guidance and encouragement that brought this work to completion and made the writing of it such a pleasurable experience.

Carole Divall, August 2018

1

Setting the Scene

In 1792 William Pitt, the prime minister, declared in his spring budget speech that he was justified in reducing the money available to the army and navy. Although he knew such predictions could be overtaken by events, he firmly believed that in no other period of history had it been possible to anticipate fifteen years of peace with such confidence. He certainly did not expect that only a year later Great Britain would be at war with France; nor could he have guessed that the wars that followed would outlast him by a decade. On 21 January 1793 the French sent their king, Louis XVI, to the guillotine. The British government responded by ejecting the French ambassador, the Marquis de Chauvelin. This gave the French the excuse to make the declaration of war for which members of the National Assembly had been agitating over several months. Already at war with Austria, Prussia, Spain and Portugal, and having invaded the territory of the Kingdom of Sardinia and the Holy Roman Empire, the Revolutionary Government now added Britain and the Dutch Republic to a lengthening list of opponents. Thus began British involvement in the French Revolutionary Wars. They would last for a further eight years. Then Europe would enjoy fourteen months of uneasy peace before the Treaty of Amiens fractured into the Napoleonic Wars.

By 1800 peace discussions were being mooted, but hindered by suspicion on all sides. The government realised there was still time to strengthen the British negotiating position through a final, viable campaign that would also serve British strategic interests.

In May 1798 Bonaparte had sailed from Toulon with an army about 18,000 strong, and with 300 ships, bound for Egypt. He landed near Alexandria at the beginning of July and then enjoyed a series of memorable victories over the Ottomans. The French had long been fascinated by Egypt. There had even been plans for the establishment of French colonies earlier in the 18th century. And Bonaparte's expedition comprised not only troops but also scientists, engineers, and artists, among them some of the most distinguished French luminaries of the day.

Bonaparte undoubtedly had personal political motives for a campaign that would burnish his reputation, and for the French there were strategic advantages to the possession of Egypt. The British navy dominated the

Mediterranean, and Bonaparte intended to challenge that domination. France was already in possession of the Ionian Islands as the result of the Treaty of Campo Formio, made with Austria in 1797 (although they temporarily lost them to the Russians in the same year). On the way to Egypt, Bonaparte seized hitherto neutral Malta from the Knights of St John, which further strengthened the French position. Most significantly, beyond Egypt lay India. Possession of the land route to the Red Sea would facilitate a campaign against the colonial underbelly of Great Britain. Nor did French ambitions end there, for they also had plans to build what would have been the first modern Suez Canal.

Although Bonaparte enjoyed success in Egypt, several events conspired to bring about a radical change both to his intentions and to the situation of the French. On the 1 August 1798, only a month after Bonaparte arrived, a British fleet under Rear Admiral Sir Horatio Nelson attacked and destroyed the French fleet at the Battle of the Nile (Aboukir Bay), thus making any return to France far more difficult to effect. Bonaparte's ambitions were finally checked at Acre in May 1799 by strong Turkish resistance, supported by Sir Sidney Smith in command of a naval detachment. Bonaparte then learnt of the political chaos in Paris. He responded by abandoning his army and returning to France, either (and it depends upon one's view of him) to save the nation or to further his own political ambitions – or possibly both.

As First Consul, the position he established for himself after his coup d'etat of 18 Brumaire, Bonaparte invited the British government to join the Austrians in discussions for an armistice. Defeats at Marengo in June, and Hohenlinden in December 1800 brought the Austrians to the negotiating table. Britain held out. By the time Addington's government joined the discussions – Pitt having resigned over the question of Catholic emancipation – a British expeditionary force had been sent to Egypt with a simple aim: eject the French. In other words, for the first time in the French Revolutionary Wars a British army had been sent on a major campaign that observed one of the critical principles of war: identify and maintain an achievable objective.

What follows is not an attempt to retell in detail the story of the Egypt Campaign 1801. Piers Mackesy's work, *British Victory in Egypt,* is a magisterial account that needs no amendment. Consequently, the events of the campaign have been presented in the form of a brief summary, followed by a more detailed examination of the key moments that defined the expedition from a British perspective. The focus is unashamedly Brito-centric since it concentrates on the forces that fought the campaign, the men who led them, and what they achieved. This was a combined operation or, as contemporaries would have called it, a *conjunct* operation. For this reason, although the main emphasis is on the troops under the command of Lieutenant General Sir Ralph Abercromby, attention is also given to the naval support of the Mediterranean fleet under Admiral Lord Keith. This was the latest of several attempts at cooperation between the two services, and undoubtedly the most successful.

In order to evaluate what is often described as a *new* British army it is necessary to consider the experiences of the army during the previous seven years. Pitt's 1792 budget speech made clear the government's confident belief that both army and navy could be cut back without endangering national security. Indeed, there was a greater fear of British radicalism and internal dissent than of foreign attack, but there was also an assumption that the militia and the various volunteer forces could be used to contain the threat at home. In order to improve the nation's finances, therefore, and in the mistaken belief that war with France could be avoided, the government did what governments have always tended to do; they reduced the size of the regular army (The same ill-judged measures were taken in 1802 after the signing of the Peace of Amiens.) The result was as predictable as the policy. The French declaration of war found Britain ill-equipped to engage in an extended continental campaign.

The problems caused by this policy will be explored in more detail elsewhere. Suffice to say, the army that was sent to Flanders in 1793 was undermanned, ill-prepared, and inadequately equipped. The army that went to Egypt eight years later was fully prepared in almost every respect for the campaign that lay ahead, although this was not entirely the work of the government. As a participant commented, they had merely sent the soldier and his sword. It was a last chance to redeem Britain's military reputation, however, and means were found by those charged with command, both at sea and on land, to take an adequately supplied and prepared force to Egypt.

2

A *New* British Army

The British Army 1793-1800

The most notable feature of the British Army in 1793 was its lack of manpower. With a total strength of 50,000 it was very much smaller than any of the major continental armies. The Austrian Army, for example, had a strength approaching a quarter of a million men. Furthermore, only about 14,000 of the British troops were home-based. Most of the remainder were serving in either the East Indies (India) or the West Indies, on board ships as marines, or posted to that convenient offshore island, Ireland. The reasons for both the limited manpower and the dispatch of such a large proportion to the colonies and Ireland are not difficult to identify. Among the general public there remained a folk memory of the Rule of the Major Generals during Cromwell's dictatorship, while Parliament saw the army as expensive and a potentially dangerous rival to its power. After all, the role of the army had been crucial to the success of the Glorious Revolution in 1688. That had been praiseworthy; but it was not difficult to imagine how the army might be mobilised again to threaten the organs of government. Thus it was sensible to keep the army small and dispersed; the colonies needed protecting from Britain's rivals, and Ireland seemed to be in a permanent state of unrest.

The disadvantage of this policy was equally obvious. Whenever Great Britain went to war there was a desperate search for manpower; and in 1793 Britain was being drawn into a war where the armies would no longer be the relatively small, highly trained instruments of royal power. Europe was about to embark on total war, initiated in the first instance by the French *levée en masse*.

In addition to these fundamental reasons for restricting the size, and thus the power, of the army, there was also the question of quality. As Henry Bunbury remembered:

> Our army was lax in its discipline, entirely without system, and very weak in numbers…there was no uniformity of drill or movement; professional pride was rare; professional knowledge more so.[1]

---

1   Sir Henry Bunbury, *Narratives of Some Passages of the Great War with France 1799-1810* (London: Peter Davies Ltd, 1927), p.xv.

Although there may be some exaggeration here, there is no question that after the final defeat in North America in 1783 very little attention was given to improving the army. Yes, David Dundas had published his *Principles of Military Movements* in 1788, which led to the issuing of *Rules and Regulations for the formations, field exercises and movements of his Majesty's forces* in 1792. These were later enforced by the Duke of York as commander-in-chief and brought to an end a colonel's power to exercise his troops by whatever method he thought best, but it would be several years before any positive results could be ascertained. Egypt would supply the answer. Furthermore, a literal application of the eighteen manoeuvres, which were the basis of the new drill, went against the lessons learnt in North American which advocated a looser kind of soldiering, known as the American system (against the German system). Out of that would grow the new approach to light infantry.

When France declared war on Great Britain on 1 February 1793 the shortage of troops immediately became apparent. The first troops sent to the Austrian Netherlands (subsequently referred to as Belgium) to act with the Austrians, Prussians and Dutch were the first battalions of the three Foot Guard regiments. These were the king's own household troops, and kept in fine condition for that reason. They were followed by three line battalions, two of which were considered, even by the Adjutant General, quite unfit for service. He felt compelled to apologise to the British commander-in-chief, the Duke of York, admitting that a considerable number of these troops were undisciplined and raw recruits, and wondering how any use could be made of them until they had learnt the business of soldiering.

Harry Calvert, one of York's aides-de-camp, observed when he first set eyes on these troops that they would not cope with the rigours of campaigning because they were either old men or boys, in both cases too weak and too undersized to be effective soldiers. As for some later reinforcements, they resembled nothing so much as Falstaff's army or the French *Carmagnole*. Another observer remarked that because of the desperate need for men the very dregs of London had been swept up. It is no wonder that they were always on the edge of indiscipline. Not surprisingly, York had no choice but to keep such troops out of action until they had undergone some systematic training. The government, of course, thought York had adequate numbers to operate effectively with the Austrians and Prussians (both receiving British subsidies, for this would be Britain's principal purpose in the early coalitions of the war) and to drive the French out of Belgium.

It is also little wonder that in 1793 the troops brought into the ranks by recruiting sergeants and crimps were so inadequate. The army was for the most part the choice of destitute and desperate man, even if as the war progressed finer feelings become apparent in the many journals and letters that were subsequently published. Taken overall, it was not an attractive life. Although a man was clothed and fed, he led a peripatetic existence, billeted on an unwilling populace, particularly innkeepers, because barracks were considered to constitute a dangerous concentration of troops. Again, later experience would change this attitude. He could be subject to fearsome punishment at the whim of his colonel, although it must be pointed out that not all colonels were floggers, and he could be sent to that graveyard of the British soldier, the Caribbean.

As for the officers, social standing, which suggested an interest in the welfare of the country, was considered more significant than ability. In 1793 there was an influx of enthusiastic but inexperienced and untrained young officers. Furthermore, 'The regimental officers in those days were, as well as their men, hard drinkers, and the latter, under the loose discipline, were much addicted to marauding, and to acts of licentious violence' which the officers were loth to control, or incapable of controlling.[2] Nor were those officers who recruited for rank likely to be too choosy about the material they brought into the ranks.

Furthermore, there was little effective direction from the top. In peacetime there was no commander-in-chief. The secretary at war lacked ministerial status, and the departments that were his responsibility were mired in incompetence and corruption. Even when, at the outbreak of war, the government needed to appoint a commander in chief of the armed forces, they chose a septuagenarian, Lord Amherst, whom one contemporary described as a log of wood whose stupidity and incapacity were past belief. It would be another two years before he was replaced by Prince Frederick, Duke of York, who, although he had disappointed as a field commander, proved to be an excellent administrator.

Not surprisingly, the small British force which fought in the Low Countries during the War of the First Coalition, supplemented by the king's other subjects, the Hanoverians, and some Hessian mercenaries, proved no match for the French. Despite the chaos of the Revolution, the French managed to combine the revolutionary fervour of their troops with effective fighting skills within a remarkably short space of time. But France had a Lazare Carnot: Britain did not. The British troops were brave and enthusiastic, but they were often undisciplined and buckled under adversity. To make matters worse, large numbers were lost to disease in the West Indies, 50 percent being a conservative estimate of the attrition rate, while India and the later acquisition of Ceylon and the Cape of Good Hope drained away even more of the army's resources. As a result, when troops were required for Britain's next continental adventure, in North Holland in 1799, there were simply not enough of them to meet the country's obligations to their Russian allies for the joint campaign. The only solution was to use newly raised and untested battalions like the 90th and the 92nd, create second battalions, and supplement the existing battalions with volunteers from the militia, drawn in by the promise that they would not have to serve beyond Europe. Previously, Militia volunteers had been given no such guarantee, with the result that very few were prepared to transfer to the regular army.

The 1799 campaign did not last long enough for the newcomers to bed down, but one man at least recognised their potential. After the army had been evacuated from North Holland, Lieutenant General Sir Ralph Abercromby wrote to Henry Dundas, the Secretary for War, that in the spring he would

---

2   Bunbury, *Narratives*, p.xxi.

have a fine army as long as the brigades were put under the command of major generals who were capable of instructing young officers and training soldiers. Abercromby also wrote to his friend, Alexander Hope, that the men from the militia were superior to those recruited straight into the ranks of the regular army. They understood the use of arms, and could move tolerably well. Their only fault was that they were not accustomed to subordination. He believed that they must be led to it by degrees. On no account must they be treated with too much harshness and severity. Many of these men, whose value Abercromby had been able to judge during the expedition to North Holland, would comprise the *new* British army that he would take to Egypt eighteen months later.

Political Preparation

The armies for the Flanders campaign in 1793 and the Anglo-Russian campaign in North Holland in 1799 were assembled in what might best be described as an *ad hoc* fashion. This had some justification in 1793. Pitt had been anxious to avoid war with France because his prime purpose was to reduce the national debt. In 1799, though, it was obvious that the lesson Flanders taught, that such *ad hoc* forces would not be able to match the unlimited manpower and new methods of war practised by the French, had not been learnt. It was all very well taking men in from the militia but, without giving them the time and training to embed themselves in the practices of the regular army, they might have enthusiasm but they would always lack relevant experience.

An expedition against the Batavian Republic, the Dutch now being a satellite of France, was a crucial element in the foreign secretary, Lord Grenville's carefully constructed strategy as the War of the Second Coalition gathered momentum. He envisaged an Austro-Russian attack on eastern France from Switzerland, and an Anglo-Russian advance through Belgium to threaten northern France. While Grenville had focused on securing Russian cooperation and Pitt, Grenville, and Dundas, the secretary for war, had debated where the expedition should actually land, the issue of manpower was left to take care of itself. As a result, the volunteers from the militia joined their new regiments only weeks before embarkation and officers were required to spend their time trying to integrate the newcomers into the existing units. The surprise is how well they performed, as noted above, and how considerable was their potential. Abercromby knew that experienced generals could teach the importance of obedience to orders without crushing the qualities of independence which made them superior to the dregs that constituted so much of the army. After all, who would wish to serve in an army that had enjoyed so little success?

The situation of the army that landed in Egypt in March 1801 was notably different from those that were hurried to the Low Countries in 1793 and 1799. Thanks to political and military developments across Europe, there was time and opportunity to prepare them for the campaign that lay ahead.

The Second Coalition was never fully secure because the participants had such differing objectives in addition to their joint aim to drive the French back behind their natural frontiers. The Russians under their notoriously unpredictable ruler, Tsar Paul I, were difficult allies. The Anglo-Dutch operations in Holland ended in bitter Russian recriminations, not entirely without justification. Austrian concerns about French intentions on the Rhine (which France had long regarded as a natural frontier) led to bad feeling as the Russians believed themselves abandoned in Switzerland, again not without justification. Grenville's hope that a joint Austro-Russian force would operate under Austrian staff officers came to naught when the Tsar pulled his troops out of the coalition. Worse still, he seemed increasingly inclined to come to some sort of understanding with the French, a situation which that clever operator, Napoleon Bonaparte, knew how to exploit.

As Grenville's strategy unravelled, Dundas was able to advocate his preferred method of fighting the French. Instinctively opposed to coalitions and suspicious of the commitment of continental allies, he argued for a colonial war to beggar the French or, at the very least, a limited operation with a clear objective, fought solely in British interests. He looked towards the Caribbean, where there had been some British success, and also considered Spain, France's ally, as a power that might easily be distracted from Europe. Spanish possessions in South American were vulnerable; the colonies were on the verge of rebellion. However, there was another possibility. As already indicated, the French occupation of Egypt, with its implicit threat to India, would eventually allow Dundas to realise his belief that although France might be invincible in Europe, her adventure against the Turks made her far more assailable.

Before a campaign to eject the French from Egypt became the preferred goal, however, it was agreed that a British force should be sent to the Mediterranean to threaten the French there, although precisely how to effect this beyond cooperating with the Austrians was never established. Another force was to create a diversion by taking Belle Île, off the coast of Brittany. Again, scarce resources were being dissipated. Yet before either force could achieve anything, one man completely transformed the situation; Napoleon Bonaparte abandoned his 'beloved Egyptians', and landed in France. Having established himself as First Consul, he then determined to break the coalition by taking war to the Austrians on the Rhine and in Northern Italy.

Bonaparte's intervention required a complete reworking of British policy, with the result that when the Mediterranean force arrived in Minorca in July 1800, complementing the troops who had taken the island from the Spanish at the end 1798, its specific purpose was to support the Austrians in Italy, where they were now under serious threat. The Belle Île expedition lingered as a possibility, and 5,000 troops were sent to Quiberon Bay in preparation for its seizure. Eventually, in September, the attack was abandoned even as the men prepared for the landings. These troops were then sent to Minorca.

The original commander of the Mediterranean force was Lieutenant General Sir Charles Stuart, who had taken Corsica from the French in 1794 and Minorca from the Spanish in 1798. He was a talented soldier, but possessed of a difficult personality. There had been serious differences of opinion during the assembling of the force, mainly because his choice of personnel was not acceptable to York as commander-in-chief. This had caused Stuart to offer his resignation, which was not accepted. When he discovered that after taking Malta from the French he was to hand it over to a Russian garrison, in an attempt to sweeten the Tsar who saw himself as the protector of the Knights of St John, he once again threatened to resign. This time he was taken at his word.

In his place Dundas appointed the famously even-tempered Abercromby to the Mediterranean command. This was probably fortuitous. Abercromby was more likely to co-operate without friction with Admiral Lord Keith, commander-in-chief of the Mediterranean fleet, who was as famous as Stuart for the prickliness of his character. As already noted, Abercromby also understood how to turn men, particularly the independent-minded men from the militia, into soldiers. Circumstances would enable him to demonstrate this talent. They would also give him the opportunity to demonstrate that, properly prepared, the British soldier could prove himself a match for the French, even the French veterans of Napoleon's first Italian campaign.

Abercromby in Command

Abercromby did not reach Minorca until 22 June 1800. Something of a Jonah, his previous attempt to reach the island had been frustrated by the weather. When he did finally arrive, he found there 10,000 men whom the governor, General Henry Fox, was preparing to embark for Genoa, which had recently been taken by the Austrians but was now reported to be threatened by the French. There was also some idea that British troops could land at various points on the coast of Italy to create diversions that would distract the French and help the Austrians. Interestingly, this would have required the application of light infantry tactics, the value of which thinking officers like Abercromby already appreciated. Abercromby sailed with his new command for what proved a fruitless enterprise. Not only was Genoa in French hands but also on 12 June Bonaparte inflicted an overwhelming defeat on the main Austrian army at Marengo. The Austrians were now beyond British help.

Abercromby brought the troops back to Minorca, where he was surprised to discover the newly arrived Colonel Lord Dalhousie with the two-battalion 20th Foot and the single-battalion 2nd, 36th, 82nd, and 92nd, all transferred from Belle Île. It was obvious that either the politicians in London had been caught on the wrong foot by Bonaparte's lightning campaign across the Alps or they already had something else in mind. Abercomby received no orders which might have clarified the situation, however. After a brief visit to Malta, where Colonel Thomas Graham was blockading the French garrison in Valletta, Abercromby set about readying his troops for action. He assumed there would be action and was waiting for a response from Dundas to his dispatches that he hoped would tell him where that action was to take place.

His first step was to organise his force into two divisions, each of two brigades. The first was under the command of Major General the Honourable

John Hely-Hutchinson, a friend of long-standing from those early days in Flanders. Major General John Moore was in command of the second division. He was also a particularly trusted friend who had served with Abercromby in the West Indies and North Holland and shared many of his attitudes to soldiering.

Abercromby then announced in the first of a series of pertinent general orders that he intended to conduct a general review of the troops, commencing on 9 August. This was a forewarning to the officers commanding battalions on the island that they should have the troops ready for inspection by that date. In the interim period Abercromby travelled the length and breadth of Minorca to inspect the troops in the most remote postings. By this means, combined with the general review, he hoped to be able to decide how he could make the best use of the various units under his command; in other words, which of them were best fitted for active service and which should remain in garrison on Minorca.

A feature of Abercromby's style of command was that he gave praise wherever he could, while not hesitating to offer criticism when it was required. As he reviewed the troops, he found much to commend, particularly in relation to what he obviously considered vital elements of effective soldiering: uniformity, steadiness under arms and cleanliness. He then enjoined Hely-Hutchinson and Moore to institute occasional field days, both to give the men much-needed exercise and to enable the practice of a few simple manoeuvres in order to attain exactness and precision. He further advocated firing with blank cartridge at order, so that they would become accustomed to the free use of their arms when encumbered with their necessaries.

One serious shortcoming that Abercromby did notice, however, was what he described as a frequent failure among the men to show proper respect to their officers, both on and off duty. Battalion commanders were therefore required to instruct the men in the appropriate *compliments* that should be paid to officers of different ranks, with the threat of punishment should they fail to observe them. This approach relates, of course, to Abercromby's concern about the men from the militia to whom subservience did not come naturally, but it also reflects his awareness that only a disciplined army where the sequence of command was fully understood could behave well in all circumstances.

Another issue, which seems trivial in itself but demonstrates Abercromby's view that all the prescribed rules of service had to be observed if discipline were to be maintained, concerned regimental bandsmen. He noticed that there was some deviation from what was perfectly correct, in that some battalions had too many bandsmen and were employing NCOs as musicians. Others listed children as privates. He stipulated that only one private from each company should be taken into the band, with only one sergeant as bandmaster. As for the sons of soldiers, it was acceptable to enlist them as drummers and fifers, but never as privates. As stated, this may seem of little moment for a general who was expecting to receive orders for an ambitious campaign (Abercromby knew of Dundas's plans for an attack on Spanish South America), but again it demonstrates his recognition that if discipline was not observed in minor matters, it could not be expected in more crucial areas of soldiering. It also indicated his belief that officers, however senior, were not exempt from the regulations of the army.

At the same time that he was enforcing training and the requirements of service, Abercromby issued other general orders which demonstrated care for the men's comfort and welfare. When he arrived back at Port Mahon after the fruitless voyage to the Italian coast and discovered the 4,000 men brought by Lord Dalhousie, his immediate concern was that sheds should be fitted out to accommodate at least some of these troops, and that they should then be rotated so that all of them would spend some time ashore until permanent quarters were found for them.

He was also unhappy with the way the men wore their knapsacks, which he recognised was potentially dangerous, so he took one away and experimented with the positioning of the straps until he had discovered how to ensure the least pressure across a man's chest. He further insisted that the contents, neatly packed, should be limited to essentials. These he listed as a blanket, two shirts, one pair of shoes, two pairs of socks, a razor, comb, brushes, blacking-ball, and soap. Anything else specified by the King's Regulations, including great coats, was to be packed in some suitable container and left with the heavy baggage. Abercromby had experience of men struggling under the weight of over-full knapsacks, particularly during the retreat to North Germany at the end of the Flanders campaign when he commanded the rear-guard. That had been the occasion when he witnessed how easily order was lost and how discipline broke down when all hope of success had died in the desperation of a retreat.

Perhaps most significantly of all, bearing in mind his thoughts on the training of recruits, Abercromby observed that several of the battalions ought to be considered as newly raised because of the number of militia volunteers and other newcomers in their ranks. For that reason, all officers, from ensigns to generals, needed to pay the greatest care and attention to the welfare of their troops. As he pointed out, their very lives might depend upon those troops on some future occasion.

On 25 August the sloop HMS *Termagant* arrived from England with the dispatches that informed Abercromby of his next objective. Because of the thoroughness with which he had conducted his review of the troops during the preceding month, he was able to announce the following day that both battalions of the 17th, along with the 20th, 36th, 82nd from the Belle Île expedition, and the Ancient Irish Fencibles would remain in garrison on Minorca under the command of Brigadier General Kenneth Mackenzie, whom he already recognised as an excellent trainer of men, while he chose to take with him two Belle Île battalions, the 2nd and the 92nd. Major General Hely-Hutchinson was appointed second-in-command. For the organisation of these battalions, which would form the basis of the army that would eventually land in Egypt, see Appendix II.

The troops embarked on 28 and 29 September, still ignorant of their eventual destination which proved to be Cadiz. This was part of a plan conceived by the government to destroy the naval resources of France's ally, Spain. The inspiration for attacks on Cadiz and Ferrol belonged to Dundas, and was based on the reasonable premise that Bonaparte would exploit the naval resources of both Spain and the Batavian (Dutch) Republic in order to challenge British sea power. The Dutch navy had been dealt a double blow: Duncan's victory at Camperdown in 1797 and Mitchell's seizure of the Texel fleet two years later. Now it was Spain's turn. In the event, the expedition to Ferrol, under Lieutenant General Sir James Pulteney, had already been aborted before Abercromby set sail from Minorca.

A final general order, of 30 September, thanked the Lieutenant Governor of Minorca, General Henry Fox, who had been Abercromby's companion in arms in Flanders, for the attention he had given to the wellbeing of the troops, and the care he had taken to find suitable accommodation for them. Although Abercromby had directed the preparation of the troops, Fox had cooperated in every respect, as senior officers tended to do with the equable Scottish general.

The first stop was Gibraltar, where the fleet arrived in the second week of September. Pulteney's Ferrol force arrived on 19 September, comprising the 2/1st, 9th, 13th, 1/27th, 2/27th, 52nd, 1/54th, 2/54th and 79th, and was quickly absorbed into Abercromby's command, giving him over 20,000 men. By 3 October the fleet was off Cadiz. Three days later everything was set for an attack ashore and the first troops were embarking in the landing craft when they were recalled by a signal gun. The following day orders were again given for embarkation and were again rescinded. Like that against Ferrol, the attack on Cadiz was abandoned, for reasons that are not completely clear. There seems little doubt that yellow fever was raging in Cadiz, but there is also evidence to suggest that Admiral Keith had not previously appreciated the difficulties of wind and tides off Cadiz, which meant he could not guarantee being able to stay close inshore in order to re-embark the army.

Two things emerged from this setback which had implications for the future. Keith, always determined to make sure that any failure would not reflect on him, had refused to commit himself on the question of re-embarkation even when Abercromby pursued him to his cabin. He insisted that the general must make the decision whether to proceed and, by implication, take the responsibility for failure. More positively, though, the spirits of the men had been high throughout, their disappointment palpable when they realised there would be no action. Abercromby was in command of a force that was eager to go into battle.

Seven of Pulteney's battalions, the two-battalion 27th and 54th, the 2/1st, and the single-battalion 13th and 79th, now joined Abercromby's force, the remainder being sent to Lisbon. There followed three weeks of uncomfortable inactivity in overcrowded and unseaworthy transports. After water had been taken on board at Tetuan and the fleet had suffered the dangers of a violent storm which scattered the ships, the most damaged vessels put in for repair and the rest sailed aimlessly off Gibraltar. No decisions could be made until dispatches arrived from England.

Even before the raid on Cadiz was aborted, the government was already considering what next to do with Abercromby's force. Dundas seized the moment and began to press urgently for an expedition to Egypt, even hijacking Cabinet meetings to make his point. At the same time, the preparatory talks about a possible armistice, between France and Austria and France and Britain, were dragging on. If successful, they would be the prelude to peace negotiations, when Egypt would be a vital factor in the subsequent bargaining. Bonaparte, however, was demanding impossible conditions, including a naval armistice and access to the French garrison on Malta, which was still under blockade. Had he known it, he was inadvertently strengthening Dundas's argument for a campaign in Egypt.

Although Grenville was focused on preserving the coalition, Pitt finally came out in favour of Egypt. Like Dundas, he recognised that removing the French was vital to the balance of power in the eastern Mediterranean. On 27 October Abercromby and Keith received dispatches which ordered them to prepare for an expedition to Egypt in alliance with the Ottoman Turks. Dundas's strategy was straightforward. Abercromby's force would attack Alexandria and then march on to Cairo, while a force from India would also advance on Cairo, from the Red Sea. In Dundas' imagination, this two-pronged attack would force the French to capitulate, so that by the end of the year they would be on their way back to France. Dundas, even after seven years of war, had little idea how long it took to set up a campaign. Providing soldiers and swords was indeed as far as it went according to his thinking. The need for horses, waggons, and all the other necessary paraphernalia lay outside his understanding.

At this point it is necessary to consider a crucial issue which divided military thinking at the time. The two contrasting approaches to tactics, as already noted, were popularly known as the American and the German systems. The war against the American colonists had demonstrated the value of light infantry, sharpshooters armed with rifles, operating in loose order. Advocates of this system, such as Generals Charles Cornwallis and Charles O'Hara, were inclined to scorn the alternative German system, based on the principles of Frederick the Great, which emphasised formation perfected by regular drill. Abercromby, who had not fought in the American War, had certainly urged David Dundas to publish his *Principles of Military Movements*, but he had also come to appreciate the benefit of light infantry, firstly in Flanders and then in the West Indies, although in both cases the practitioners had been Germans, essentially mercenaries in British service. While he was on Minorca his expectation was that he might still be taking his army to the Italian coast or, possibly, the Caribbean or South America, none of them ideal country for the tightly regulated manoeuvres of the *Principles*, but the terrain in each case could be exploited by light infantry. As a result, he had introduced some light infantry manoeuvres into the soldiers' training. Egypt had a very different terrain, however, suitable for large-scale cavalry attacks. The French had plenty of cavalry, whereas Abercromby at this point had only about a thousand, and not enough horses to mount them. In such circumstances the German system came into its own. Men could be drilled to stand against cavalry attacks, to form square, and to march in square. In other words, drill would be based on Dundas's *Principles,* although Abercromby recognised that the eighteen manoeuvres needed to be simplified for use in the heat and confusion of battle, a task he set himself. He was fortunate that he was granted the opportunity to implement his ideas.

3

Final Preparations

As soon as the news of his destination reached Abercromby, he sent a request to Lord Elgin, ambassador to the Ottoman Empire in Constantinople, to procure horses and mules for the expedition. He also sent his quartermaster general, Colonel Robert Anstruther, to Rhodes and the assistant quartermaster general, Lieutenant Colonel George Murray, to Jaffa, the former to collect supplies and the latter to make contact with the Turks and assess their capabilities. The Turks were crucially important to Dundas's strategy, which was based on their willing co-operation. The main Turkish force, which was under the command of the Grand Vizier, was to cross the Syrian and Sinai deserts and advance into Egypt. There was a second, smaller, Turkish force under the Captain Pacha which was thought to be closer. Anstruther had some success in his mission, although the Turks proved dilatory, but Murray expressed serious concerns about them as active allies. There seemed to be no order in their military arrangements; not even musters to provide accurate numbers. Later, Moore was sent to discover more about the Grand Vizier's force. What he discovered merely reinforced the opinion Murray had already given, that it was not in a state of readiness for action and could not be depended upon.

Abercromby had not forgotten his experience of trying to work with the Austrians in Flanders and the Russians in Holland. He had already decided, therefore, that the British and the Turks should operate as separate forces, although he had made clear to them that he was prepared to land at whatever place best suited them, either Damietta or Aboukir Bay. Now it seemed as if he and his army would be on their own, initially if not for the whole campaign. Nevertheless, he tried to co-ordinate his plans with the Turks, and was careful to keep them informed of his intentions, which finally crystallised into a determination to land near Aboukir Bay.

Before the departure for Egypt, five hundred sick were left in Gibraltar, and the 2/27th, decimated by fever, was sent to Lisbon in the ships in which they had embarked for the Mediterranean. Then the fleet set sail for its first stopping point, Malta. The original intention had been to stop over at Port Mahon before sailing on to Malta, but Abercromby then changed his mind since it would be a waste of valuable time. He had no expectation of fulfilling Dundas's timetable, but he still hoped to avoid the heat of an Egyptian summer. The plan was changed so that only the ships most urgently in need of repair after the storms off Tetuan visited Minorca. Those who did sail there found the place in a bustle of activity as ships were prepared for a long voyage. It was at this point that the troops realised their destination was Egypt, information that seems to have created great excitement. It was one thing to fight the Spanish: to fight the French was quite another matter, and a challenge to be relished.

The voyage to Malta was disrupted by yet more storms but by the third week of November all the undamaged naval ships and transports had reached the island, while the Minorcan contingent arrived soon after. For Private Daniel Nicol of the 92nd, Malta was a place he associated with several stirring historical events, not the least of them being the shipwreck of the apostle Paul, so he remained on deck to enjoy the experience of arriving in a place with such strong associations. He was not alone in his sense of history. It is also worth noting that this regiment, the Gordon Highlanders, had just received 200 volunteers, mainly from the Caithness and Inverness Fencibles. It was fortunate, therefore, that circumstances allowed them time to bed down in their new unit.

Not all the troops could be accommodated ashore, but they were landed in rotation to be exercised and so that the transports could be cleaned. They were also supplied with fresh beef and vegetables, which Abercromby considered vital for the maintenance of good health. To the men's delight, prices proved surprisingly cheap in Malta. It is no wonder, therefore, that a sergeant of artillery managed to get so drunk that he nearly drowned when rescuing a cat from the rough sea. According to Benjamin Miller's own account, it may not have been raining cats and dogs that day, but the rain was so heavy it was washing cats and dogs into the sea.

The French garrison holed up in Valletta had finally surrendered on 4 September. This released the two British battalions, the 30th and the 89th, which had been involved in the blockade. Abercromby inspected them, bestowed generous praise on both but particularly on the 30th, and decided to take them to Egypt. They were replaced in garrison by the 1/27th, now as weakened by fever as the regiment's junior battalion, and the 40th and the 63rd, both regiments that had large numbers of Europe-only militia volunteers in their ranks. Europe only service, which precluded being sent to the dreaded Caribbean where a battalion could expect to lose half its manpower in one season's campaigning, had continued to lure militiamen into the regular army; but for the present purpose, Egypt was considered to lie outside Europe. Such was the eagerness for action which now informed Abercromby's force, however, that the men of the two-battalion 40th volunteered *en masse* for Egypt. Abercromby chose to take the four flank companies, but also praised the whole regiment for its zeal. It also meant he could take with him Colonel Brent Spencer, of whom he had a high opinion based on his conduct in the Helder campaign.

Dundas had intended that the expedition should sail directly from Malta to Egypt but there was still a lack of landing craft and supplies, to say nothing of the means of moving the supplies. Furthermore, Elgin had yet to acquire a sufficient number of horses, and no provision had been made for accommodating the sick. Abercromby's contingent finally departed from Malta on 20 December, followed soon afterwards by Hely-Hutchinson's contingent, and both sailed via Rhodes to Marmaris Bay, there to await the arrival of boats, supplies and horses. The last became even more crucial when the 12th and 26th Light Dragoons arrived. Only the officers had horses. It could certainly be argued that the government should have overseen the proper provision of all these commodities when the decision was made to attack the French in Egypt but it is unlikely that Abercromby was surprised when they failed to do so. He had yet to be involved in a well-supplied British campaign.

One strange point that emerges from the journals of the time, and there are a fair number of them, is the sense of history already remarked upon. It was felt not only by some of the officers but also by some of the men. An officer on the 2nd (Queen's), as the British ships sailed close to where the fateful sea-battle of Lepanto had been fought over 200 years before, was struck by the irony that then Muslims and Christians had been opposed to each other; now Muslims and Christians were allies against a common foe. Later, a soldier of the 92nd wondered at finding himself in the lands associated with some of the greatest figures of ancient history.

As the expedition was a *conjunct* operation, the most critical time would be when the army landed with the vital assistance of the navy. At Den Helder Abercromby had witnessed the chaos that ensued when the navy failed to grasp the importance of the troops landing in order of battle. They had been lucky on that occasion that only a relatively small Dutch force opposed them. He knew by report that Belle Île had been the same, with army and navy failing to function as a genuinely conjunct force. At Cadiz Admiral Keith's had refused to conduct himself as the senior naval officer of a combined operation should. His failure to make those decisions which pertained to his role had paralysed his officers as they waited for the instructions that Keith was determined not to give. This had reduced the whole expedition to farce. As a result, Abercromby had made up his mind that neither the naval mismanagement of Den Helder nor the contumely of the senior naval officer should hamper the landings in Egypt, particularly as the French could be counted upon to offer a fierce opposition and take ruthless advantage of any confusion.

Abercromby may well have been one of the few senior army officers who could cope with a man of Keith's temperament. Indeed, he had promised himself before his expedition to the West Indies in 1796 that he would never quarrel with an admiral, such behaviour being inexcusable according to his personal code of conduct. That resolution had been simple to observe with Admirals Christian and Harvey. On this occasion, having had his request for a change of commander of the Mediterranean fleet turned down, he simply bypassed Keith. In this he had the support of Keith's second-in-command, Rear Admiral Sir Richard Bickerton. Also, when the assistant captain of Keith's flagship, the *Foudroyant,* was appointed captain, the new assistant captain was William Yonge, formerly Principal Agent for Transports, an expert in troop movements. It was also agreed that Captain Alexander Cochrane, who had exercised the same responsibility at Cadiz and proved himself a man with whom Abercromby could work comfortably, should be in command of organising the boats and getting the troops ashore. To ensure that the needs of the army took priority, though, Anstruther was ordered to brief Cochrane throughout. Fortunately, the two men soon demonstrated that they could work harmoniously together.

The stay in Marmaris Bay allowed Abercromby time to do the one thing that had never been possible before, practise the landings. There was a particular problem with the chosen landing place of Aboukir Bay, however; chosen because of its proximity to Alexandria, where half the French army was posted. The bay was shallow as far as seven miles out. The usual practice when landing an army required the naval boats to bring the first wave of troops ashore, after which the sailors would row back to the ships as quickly as possible to collect the second wave. Any delay would give the enemy too much time to overwhelm the first wave before the second wave had any chance of supporting them. This arrangement would not work at Aboukir. The interval between the two landings would be long enough to allow the defenders to overpower the first wave before reinforcements arrived. And the oarsmen would be so exhausted by the distance they would have rowed to bring the first wave ashore that they would struggle to row back to collect the second wave and then bring them ashore. In fact, the whole operation would be dangerously protracted.

Consequently, an alternative approach was devised by which the second wave would be brought close inshore in cutters and similar craft to wait their turn in the landing craft. The first wave would be rowed from further back, past the waiting second wave, and landed. The oarsmen would then waste little time bringing in the second wave. Furthermore, with two men of talent like Cochrane and Anstruther working closely together Abercromby could be confident that the troops would land in order of battle, thus avoiding the fatal confusion which would give the French the chance to pounce.

Such a system could only work with repeated practise, which the delay at Marmaris Bay made possible. The first rehearsal, involving two brigades, took place on 21 January and proceeded perfectly, so that the troops were in battalion order within minutes of landing. The process was repeated several times, with mixed results. On 2 February, for instance, a practice involving the 2nd, 3rd and 4th brigades descended into total chaos, although this may have been caused by a sudden change of plan. Cochrane had originally intended that there should be an assembly point before the landing craft rowed to the transports. On 2 February that idea was abandoned and for the first time the small boats went straight to the transports, which as noted resulted in the kind of disorder that would cause multiple casualties during an actual landing. Subsequent rehearsals eased this initial confusion, and by the time the expeditionary force was ready to depart from Marmaris every man involved in the landings, military and naval, knew exactly what he had to do.

Practising landings was not all that engaged Abercromby's attention. As was his usual custom, he drew up a code of conduct for the troops, this time placing particular emphasis on the need to respect the religion and customs of the local people, both at Marmaris and in Egypt. He was also concerned about the rising incidence of sickness and gave orders on the advice of his senior medical officer, Thomas Young, that all those unfit for duty should be camped on shore, which rapidly reduced the number of sufferers. It was not without risk, however. Even the fit men were disturbed by the sound of wild beasts after darkness fell. They and the invalids protected themselves by keeping fires alight all night.

Keith shared Abercromby's recognition that fresh beef and vegetables improved the health of soldiers and sailors, and ships were sent as far as Rhodes to purchase them. Abercromby also persuaded Keith to let the soldiers on the transports, who were actively engaged in manning the vessels, have the same rations as the sailors rather than the usual three quarters, a request that Keith willingly granted since there was no risk that it could be held against him. As on Malta, Abercromby also rotated bringing the troops ashore, while reviews and drill continued with emphasis on the manoeuvres required for Egypt as now devised, including moving rapidly and efficiently from line to square, ready to receive the inevitable attacks of the French cavalry.

There were practical matters to oversee as well. Moving supplies would be a particular challenge across the Egyptian terrain, so men were set to work constructing carriers with shafts, rather like sledges, which could be hauled by horses or by groups of men. Ammunition boxes were adapted so that they could be transported on camels. There was the normal employment of making gabions and fascines in anticipation of siege work at Alexandria and Cairo. And to keep the men busy, those with nothing else to do were given the task of making wooden mallets and tent pegs. Nor was the navy standing by. While coopers and carpenters aboard ship were producing casks and barrels, the other sailors joined the soldiers in their preparations for the campaign.

Another critical issue was water, and on 10 May Abercromby devoted a general order to the matter of an adequate supply. He had received information that suggested there were several wells between Aboukir Bay and Alexandria, while a further supply could be found by digging five or six feet deep into the bed of the Canal of Alexandria. He also knew, from his reading of Julius Caesar, that digging around date trees would reveal yet more water (Sir Sidney Smith later claimed that the idea was his, but it is likely that he and Abercromby were not the only ones to remember what Caesar had written). Nevertheless, water was too scarce a commodity to be wasted and Abercromby issued strict orders that it should be used with regularity and economy. The men must also be prepared to wash in seawater, and even cook their food in it, although he did suggest that some contrivance could be made so that the meat and vegetables were steamed rather than boiled. There was also a reminder that the native horses required far less water than British ones, no more than two or three gallons a day. As a final rejoinder to officers and men alike, he pointed out that water was of the most material consequence, for the success of the campaign depended on its availability and careful use. Perhaps he also felt a certain satisfaction that water would have to suffice in a land where alcohol was *haram* [forbidden by Allah]. The only alcohol the men would taste would be the carefully controlled rations of rum brought from the ships. Of course, this was an added advantage to campaigning in a hot climate, where the combination of alcohol and heat could, and often did, prove fatal.

Although the promised horses (which were always going to be inadequate in number) had arrived during this period of preparation, the transports to convey them to Egypt did not reach Marmaris until 16 February. With their arrival the army could finally embark for Egypt. As Colonel John Abercromby, the general's son, serving as assistant adjutant general, wrote in his diary, 'Never was there an expedition attended with more important and extraordinary circumstances. Never was the honour of the British army more at stake, or its animated exertions more required: and never was the interest of the country more deeply involved than in its ultimate success'.[1] He might have added that, based on the writings of officers and men alike, never was an army more eager to get at the enemy. The delay at Marmaris had only sharpened their appetite for action.

The commander-in-chief had done everything in his power to prepare his army for its imminent encounter with the French Army of the Orient, veterans from Bonaparte's first Italian campaign and scourge of the Turks. Only time would tell if the new British army could indeed take the fight to the enemy and win a comprehensive victory.

1   James, Lord Dunfermline, *Lieutenant-General Sir Ralph Abercromby, A Memoir* (Edinburgh: Edmondston & Douglas, 1861), pp.273-274.

4

The Army of Egypt

Much of the information that follows also appears elsewhere in the text. The duplication is deliberate since this section is designed to give a brief overview of what might be termed the dramatis personae, *the men who, either as individuals or as members of their battalion, had a role to play in the forthcoming campaign. To continue the theatrical allusion, the rank and file might be regarded as extras, there to make up the numbers, but every last one of them was crucial to British success.*

It was not the British fashion at this time to give armies territorial appendages. The army that was initially put together in rather extempore fashion to operate with the Austrians in the Mediterranean, and then to threaten the Spanish, became (as already noted) a force with a single objective, to eject the French Army of the Orient from Egypt. For that reason I have chosen to call it the *Army of Egypt* in imitation of the French convention to name their armies after the site of their service.

Furthermore, in order to understand how that objective was achieved when previously only colonial expeditions had realised any degree of success, it is relevant to examine the forces that fought in Egypt and the men who commanded them at the highest level. Nor should the naval contingent be overlooked.

The commander of the expedition, **Lieutenant General Sir Ralph Abercromby** (1734-1801), was originally intended for the law but after a period in Leipzig, where he became aware of the military methods of Frederick the Great and the Prince of Brunswick, he persuaded his father to let him pursue a military career. His was a legal family, but his younger brother and an uncle were already serving soldiers. Somewhat reluctantly, his father allowed him to break the family tradition. He joined the 3rd Dragoon Guards by purchase in 1756, which coincided with the outbreak of the Seven Years War. Two years later he went with his regiment to Germany, where he served as aide de camp to Colonel Sir William Pitt. In 1760 he transferred to the 3rd Regiment of Horse with the rank of lieutenant, was promoted to captain soon afterwards, and eventually rose to lieutenant colonel. At the outbreak of the American War of Independence he remained with his regiment in Ireland, having made clear that he would not fight in what he regarded as a civil war.

He was appointed colonel of the newly raised 103rd Foot (King's Irish Infantry) in 1781, and when the regiment was disbanded three years later he went on half-pay. This was still his situation in 1793, although in the interim he was promoted to the general list.

A man of liberal opinions, Abercromby might have been expected to sympathise with the French Revolutionaries. Yet, although he did indeed sympathise with their attempts to reform the French state, he did not approve of their methods. When France declared war on Britain in 1793 Major General Abercromby volunteered to serve and was appointed to the command of a line brigade By this time he had learnt much about the management and training of men but knew little of the battlefield. Sent to Flanders, he soon demonstrated the intrepidity and coolness that became the distinguishing marks of his active career. Whether he was commanding an inadequate line brigade or the superior troops of the Guards, whom he also led into action on several crucial occasions, he managed to get the best out of his men. During the cruel winter of 1794-1795, and the desolate retreat to Bremen, he revealed another side of his character. In command of the rear-guard, comprising the Guards but also a large number of sick, he showed a degree of humanity and concern that won him the love of all who served under him. This he was to retain until his death.

Lieutenant General Sir Ralph Abercromby. (Author's Collection).

He was one of the few senior officers of that inadequate army to emerge with his reputation burnished. His friend and distant cousin, Henry Dundas, was the minister for war and Abercromby became his commander of choice. Two expeditions to the West Indies (1796 and 1797) resulted in the conquest of St Lucia from the French and Trinidad from the Spanish, and the suppression of rebellions on St Vincent and Grenada. There followed a brief and unhappy period in Ireland, from December 1797 to April 1798, when as commander-in-chief his liberal principles and belief that the only effective army was a disciplined one brought him into conflict with the Protestant Ascendancy. His resignation, however, was immediately followed by his appointment as commander-in-chief, Scotland, at King George III's insistence. He had also enjoyed the full support of the Duke of York during this difficult time.

In 1799, during the War of the Second Coalition, he led an advance force to North Holland, held his ground during the chaotic landings at Callantsoog, and beat off a Franco-Dutch attack under *Général de Division* Brune. After York, who was in command of the main army, and the Russians had landed he became the most dependable of York's subordinates. Too cautious for some later commentators, he had a pragmatic awareness of the Dutch, based on experience gained during the previous campaign in the Low Countries; he knew they would offer no support to the Anglo-Russian force while the outcome of the campaign was in doubt. He was also conscious of the serious failings in preparation, for which the government had to take responsibility.

As the Second Coalition collapsed, friction intensified within the British cabinet. Dundas, whose areas of responsibility covered both war and the colonies, was looking beyond Europe, while Grenville, from the perspective of his role as foreign secretary, was determined to keep Austria in the war. Although Abercromby was sent to command the force stationed on Minorca, which Grenville saw as an auxiliary army to help the Austrians in northern Italy, the minister for war had more ambitious plans. When the Battle of Marengo (14 June 1800) rendered any co-operation pointless, Dundas suggested an attack either on Tenerife or against Spanish naval resources at Ferrol and Cadiz. With Bonaparte pushing for an armistice as a first step towards peace negotiations, though, Dundas recognised that French-occupied Egypt was a more urgent objective. As already seen, the Ferrol and Cadiz operations were launched but achieved nothing, whereupon Egypt became the prime target for Abercromby's army.

After the failure in Flanders, Abercromby had told Dundas that there would be no success until politicians let generals get on with the business they understood best. Abercromby, now in his 67th year, informed his family that Egypt would be his last campaign. However, with communications between London and the eastern Mediterranean taking weeks to arrive, and Dundas giving him a freer hand than he had ever previously enjoyed, it was also his first chance to demonstrate what a general could do with a good army when left to his own devices within the necessary constraints of a clearly-defined objective. As has already been described, his preparations were as thorough and meticulous as he could make them. Now the army that he had been nurturing for months finally had the chance to prove itself and justify him.

Major General John Hely-Hutchinson. (Author's Collection)

Second in command of the expedition was Dublin-born **Major General John Hely-Hutchinson** (1751-1832), a man who, like Abercromby, opted for a military career against the legal tradition of his family. He was commissioned by purchase into the 18th Light Dragoons in 1774, again like Abercromby starting his career in his early twenties which was rather later than most officers entered the army. Two years later he was a captain in the 67th Foot, eventually rising to lieutenant colonel. In 1783 he was appointed colonel of the 77th Foot (Atholl Highlanders) but the regiment was disbanded soon afterwards and Hely-Hutchinson went on half-pay for eleven years. During this time he visited the Military Academy, Strasbourg, to study French military procedures.

When in 1792 war broke out between the French on one side and the Austrians and Prussians on the other, Hely-Hutchinson visited both the French and the Prussian armies, again to further his knowledge of continental methods. He was then sent by the government to take a look at the Russians. In 1793, with Britain now involved in the war, he volunteered for service in Flanders and was on Abercromby's staff as an extra aide-de-camp. This was the beginning of a friendship that was undoubtedly cemented by their shared principles; principles which, at the time, were considered dangerously radical. Hely-Hutchinson, who had a seat in the Irish Parliament, strongly advocated Catholic emancipation and favoured union with the rest of Britain as a means of limiting the power of the Protestant Ascendancy. In 1796 he was appointed to the general list and two years later was in command of Connaught during the Rebellion. He received a sword and the thanks of the people of the province for his judicious conduct. He was second-in-command to Lieutenant General Lake at the Battle of Castlebar, when French invaders and Irish rebels defeated British regular forces. In 1799 he volunteered to serve in North Holland, and took command of Lord Cavan's brigade when Cavan was wounded.

Abercromby acknowledged Hely-Hutchinson as his second-in-command on seniority, despite the Irishman's negative view of the campaign. Abercromby himself recognised that it was a perilous undertaking but Hely-Hutchinson's pessimism was more extreme. Not only was he a more depressive character than the commander-in-chief; he was also known to lose his temper all too easily, which was unexpected in one of his thoughtful approach to soldiering. So disruptive could he be that his own brother, who had volunteered for Egypt, found him impossible to live with. Slovenly in appearance, he inspired no confidence, and also suffered from being little known to officers and men alike.

Serving as adjutant general was another man Abercromby knew well, **Brigadier General John Hope** (1765-1823). The younger son of the 2nd Earl of Hopetoun, he was commissioned into the 10th Light Dragoons in 1784, and had reached the rank of captain five years later. After a brief period as major in the 5th Foot, he was appointed lieutenant colonel of the 25th Foot in 1793, and colonel three years later. He accompanied Abercromby to the West Indies and, along with John Moore, played a prominent part in the conquest of St Lucia. The following year he served as brigadier general on Abercromby's expedition to Trinidad and Puerto Rico. He was also involved in the expedition to North Holland, as deputy adjutant general. Chosen by Abercromby to accompany him to Minorca, he was sufficiently trusted to be sent to the Austrians after Marengo to report on their situation so that a decision could be made about whether they were in a state to benefit from British support. Hope's judgement convinced Abercromby that the army of General Melas was beyond all assistance. On Minorca he was deputed, along with Moore, to carry out many of the inspections that Abercromby insisted upon as he prepared his army for action.

Hope later served in the Peninsula, firstly under Moore (1808-1809) and then under Wellington, commanding the 1st Division from 1813 to 1814. He was taken prisoner at Bayonne, days after the war officially ended. He was also involved in the disastrous expedition to Walcheren (1809).

Hope's deputy was **Colonel John Abercromby (1772-1817)**, the commander-in-chief's second son. His military career began at a very young age, in 1782, when he was notionally a cornet in the 4th Dragoons. In 1786, aged just fourteen, he was appointed ensign in the 75th Foot, lieutenant a year later and captain in 1792. Two years after that he transferred to the 94th with the rank of major, and within months was lieutenant colonel of the 112th. In 1795 he exchanged into the 53rd. His rapid rise was ascribed both to his own talents and to his father's reputation. He was with his father in Flanders, the West Indies and Ireland, serving as aide de camp, and in North Holland as his military secretary. This was a significant post because the general's short-sightedness meant he needed someone to interpret situations when a telescope alone did not give him the information he required. John was able to do this with great perspicuity. Having been promoted colonel at the beginning of 1800, he could no longer serve on his father's staff. Instead he was appointed deputy adjutant general and served under Hely-Hutchinson's direct command.

He subsequently had the misfortune to be in France at the breakdown of the Peace of Amiens in 1803, and spent five years as a prisoner at Verdun, before being exchanged for *Général de Brigade* Brenier, taken at Vimeiro. He then spent the rest of his military career in India.

Colonel Robert Anstruther (1765-1809), who served as quartermaster general, was another Scot from a background similar to the commander-in-chief's. He started his career with the 3rd Foot Guards in 1788. By 1793 he commanded a company with the rank of lieutenant colonel, as was the norm in the Guards, and fought with them in Flanders. Four years later, eager for more active service, he purchased a majority and then a lieutenant colonelcy in the 68th Foot. He served with his new regiment in the expedition to Trinidad and Puerto Rico, where he seems to have attracted the attention of Abercromby, who, as noted, had a good eye for able officers. Anstruther changed regiments yet again in 1799, once more in the hope of more active service, transferring back to the 3rd Foot Guards and back to his previous rank with them when he realised they were about to serve with the expeditionary force to North Holland. When Abercromby was given the Mediterranean command, he chose Anstruther as his quartermaster general on the basis that here was a man he knew and trusted. On Minorca, Anstruther had the time to learn that basics of his new position.

Not only that, but Anstruther also developed the confidence to voice an opinion when the need arose. As Keith vacillated about whether the troops should land at Cadiz, it was Anstruther who pointed out to Abercromby that he should really obtain something in writing from Keith, since the general was being manoeuvred into a position where he would take all the blame for failure. Anstruther knew that all the naval officers were opposed to the landing. Interestingly, Abercromby took his advice and wrote to Keith, pointing out that the expedition was a conjunct operation. This meant the admiral had to give his judgement on whether the landings were viable. Furthermore, the letter could not be ignored since failure to answer it would demonstrate his dereliction of duty. Keith finally admitted that he would advise Abercromby not to land. Anstruther's advice had forced Keith to commit himself.

Once it became clear that Egypt was the objective, Abercromby sent Anstruther to the Turks on Rhodes to establish communications with their allies. When Anstruther reported the difficulties he anticipated in persuading the Turks to appreciate the need for urgent action, Abercromby judged the report reliable and accepted that he must be prepared to act alone, particularly in the first instance. Moreover, when it eventually came, help from the Turks could prove invaluable. Abercromby was determined, though, that it would be on his terms, a resolve that he had formed after receiving Anstruther's report.

Whoever was quartermaster general during the campaign was going to be thoroughly tested. It is to Anstruther's credit, therefore, that he coped with the challenges Egypt offered, so that there are few complaints in the journals of the soldiers. He also seems to have established good relations with his naval counterparts. Like Hope, Anstruther later served in the Peninsula, at Vimeiro under Arthur Wellesley, and then under Moore's command. He died shortly before the final action at Corunna, of an inflammation of the lungs.

Anstruther's deputy was his close friend, **Lieutenant Colonel George Murray** (1772-1846) whom Anstruther himself tutored in staff work. Murray had been commissioned into the 71st Foot in 1789, and subsequently served with the 34th Foot and the 3rd Foot Guards, accompanying the latter to Flanders. During the campaign he was promoted to captain and lieutenant colonel in accordance with the dual rank held by Guards officers. In 1795 he accompanied Lord Moira to Quiberon in the second of several attempts to support the Royalists within France. Like Toulon, the expedition ultimately achieved nothing, but Murray demonstrated his administrative competence when he served on the staff of Major General Alexander Campbell. He then accompanied Abercromby to the West Indies, but within a few months had to return to Britain on health grounds. He spent two years in England and Ireland (1797-1799) on Campbell's staff. Like Anstruther, he went with the 3rd Foot Guards to North Holland, and was appointed to the quartermaster general's department. There followed a secret expedition to Java, after which he was appointed DQMG for the expedition to Egypt. Abercromby used Murray to make contact with the Turks at Jaffa. His report convinced Abercromby that he needed someone to take an even closer look at the Turkish forces, a task he deputed to John Moore.

Murray is perhaps best known for his later service as Wellington's quartermaster general in the Peninsular, although before that he was in Iberia with Moore. At Corunna he suffered the loss of his friend, Anstruther. Murray and Wellington first encountered each other during the expedition to Copenhagen in 1807, and Murray quickly impressed Wellesley, as he then was, with his staff work. Murray then served with Wellington from 1809 until 1811, when a broken collarbone brought him home, and again from 1813 to 1814. During this second period Murray became one of the few men Wellington trusted to show some independence of mind.

Although he was not on the staff, **Major General John Moore** (1761-1809) was destined to play a crucial part in the conduct of the campaign as the most

Major General John Moore.
(Author's Collection)

trusted of Abercromby's subordinates. His father was a Glasgow doctor who enjoyed the patronage of the Duke of Hamilton, and this connection undoubtedly fostered the early career of the son, after which his natural talent enabled him to impress. Moore was originally commissioned into the 51st Foot in 1776, but when he went to Nova Scotia two years later he was a lieutenant in the 82nd Foot, a regiment recently raised by the Duke of Hamilton. He made his name in 1779 when, as part of an expeditionary force to Maine, he managed to hold off an attack by a body of American Colonists until reinforcements arrived, even though his force was greatly outnumbered. In 1787 he joined the 60th Foot with the rank of major, but returned to his original regiment four years later. In 1794 he was with Charles Stuart on Corsica and was wounded at Calvi. He was appointed adjutant general and promoted to brevet colonel by Stuart. Unfortunately, like Stuart, he aroused the resentment of Sir Gilbert Elliot, the governor, and had to leave the island at 48 hours' notice. He did, however, receive the approbation of the Duke of York on his return.

Moore first met Abercromby when he was posted to the West Indies in 1795. The two men immediately established a rapport that was to last until Abercromby's death. Moore, like Hope, played a prominent part in the capture of St Lucia, and was then entrusted with command of the island after Abercromby departed for St Vincent and Grenada. He finally returned to Britain in 1797, having suffered two debilitating attacks of yellow fever. He then accompanied Abercromby to Ireland at the end of that year and was promoted to major general the following year. He supported the commander's liberal views and shared his belief that troops would only function efficiently when disciplined and kept in order. This was the very opposite of what was happening in Ireland, where they were being used by the civil powers to support the Ascendency's agenda. Moore remained in Ireland after Abercromby's resignation and during the Rebellion he refrained from the brutal excesses of many of his fellow commanders, although he was firm enough when it became necessary to disarm the local population.

Moore was recalled to England in the summer of 1799 to serve under Abercromby in North Holland. After two slight wounds, he suffered a serious injury at the Battle of Egmont. In 1800 he was with Abercromby in Minorca and from there on supported Abercromby's approach to command: discipline, training, and unremitting concern for the welfare of the troops. Like Hope, he was deputed to carry out frequent regimental inspections in the commander's name. As the start of the campaign drew closer, Abercromby sent him to Jaffa, where he saw enough of the Grand Vizier's army, the main Turkish force, to convince him they were quite unready to offer any effective co-operation in the short term. At best, they might serve a diversionary purpose, which was their role until Cairo was under siege, when they played an equal part in the final surrender of the city.

Moore is remembered principally for his dedication to the training of light infantry, the value of which he had learnt in the West Indies, and his hero's death at the Battle of Corunna in January 1809.

When considering the British Army of Egypt, it is important not to overlook the contingent coming from India under the command of **Major General David Baird** (1757-1829). He was another Scot, and the presence of so many Scots in significant positions did lead to mutterings against a Scottish cabal which had obviously been promoted by a Scottish minister for war and implemented by his Scottish commander-in-chief. Baird was commissioned into the 2nd Foot in 1772. Six years later, he transferred to command a company in the 73rd Foot. The following year his new regiment was sent to India, finally reaching Madras in 1780. They soon became involved in the Second Anglo-Mysore War. Baird was wounded and taken prisoner at the Battle of Perinbancum (August 1781) against the Mysorean leader, Hyder Ali. He and his fellow prisoners were held for three years in the most severe conditions, never knowing whether they would survive until the following morning. It was not until his release that the bullet which had lodged close to his spine was finally extracted.

In 1787 Baird returned to Britain with his regiment, now numbered the 71st, with the rank of major, and was promoted lieutenant colonel three years later. He returned to India in 1791, serving under Cornwallis. On his voyage back to Europe in 1797 he put in at the Cape of Good Hope, recently taken from the French, who had in turn taken control of it from the Dutch. He was persuaded by the governor to remain there with the position of brigadier general in order to head off what was threatening to be a mutiny against the military commander, David Dundas. By 1799, though, he was back in India with the rank of major general and led the storming party at Seringapatam.

Major General David Baird.
(Author's Collection)

Baird was both a hard-bitten soldier and a man who harboured grudges. Indeed, his own mother, when informed that her son was a prisoner, remarked that she pitied the man chained to her Davie. These two traits of character fostered his resentment against Arthur Wellesley, whose military career was being unashamedly furthered by his brother, Richard, the governor-general. When Baird was appointed to command the force for Egypt, Wellesley should have been his second-in-command but illness prevented what would undoubtedly have been a potentially difficult state of affairs.

Baird commanded an independent force during Moore's Peninsular campaign. He lost his arm at the Battle of Corunna, which brought his active career to an end.

The British Forces

Lieutenant General Abercromby organised his army in the normal British fashion of the time. Consequently, the force that landed at Aboukir on 8 March 1801 comprised six brigades of infantry, one designated the Reserve, and one of cavalry. Each was commanded by a brigadier, most of them men with the rank of major general, although the fourth and fifth were commanded by colonels. The artillery was also under the command of a colonel. For a full order of battle, see Appendix II

The Guards Brigade

Major General George Ludlow (1758-1842), in command, was the 2nd son of the 1st Earl Ludlow in the Irish peerage. He served with the 1st Foot Guards from 1778 until being placed on the general list in 1795. In 1781 he accompanied detachments from his regiment to North America and a few months later was with Cornwallis at the surrender of Yorktown. At the outbreak of the French Revolutionary Wars 1793 he went to Flanders in command of one of the light companies which had recently been added to the battalion. The following year he lost an arm in the action at Roubaix. Four years later, and now a major general, he was given command of the 2nd Brigade of Guards comprising the 1/Coldstream Guards and the 1/3rd Foot Guards. He held this position first at the aborted attacks on Ferrol and Cadiz (1800), and then in Egypt, although he was later transferred to the 1st Brigade at the instigation of the Guards officers themselves (Ludlow had been given the colonelcy of a line regiment and the Guards insisted they had the right to be commanded only by one of their own).

After the return from Egypt he served as a divisional commander during the expeditions to Hanover (1805) and Copenhagen (1807). He succeeded his brother as 3rd Earl Ludlow in 1811.

Both the **Coldstreamers** and the **3rd Foot Guards** had been with Abercromby in the Low Countries (1793-1795), much of the time under his direct command. They had also been in North Holland in 1799 and were involved in the disorderly landings at Callantsoog, again under Abercromby's command. As the King's personal troops, the Guards regiments were always kept up to strength and in fine fighting fettle, a point demonstrated by their conduct during the retreat in the winter of 1794 and noted by Moore when he surveyed the battalions in the advance force at Den Helder.

> Coldstream Guards: blue facings, plain lace in pairs
> 3rd Foot Guards: blue facings, plain lace in threes
> Total strength as of 7 March: 1,578 (766 + 812)

The 1st Brigade

Major General Eyre Coote (1762-1823) was another of the several Irish brigadiers involved in the expedition. He was commissioned into the 27th Foot in 1774 and was with them in North America, where his active service was brought to an end by Cornwallis's surrender at Yorktown. By 1793 he had risen to the rank of lieutenant colonel of the 70th Foot. He served in the West Indies, first with Grey (1794) and then with Abercromby. Appointed major general in 1798, he next commanded an expedition to Ostend. Its objective was to cut the sluices there and flood the countryside. This was achieved, although Coote was seriously wounded. When contrary winds prevented re-embarkation, he and the survivors of his force were taken prisoner, although he was subsequently exchanged. He was given brigade command in the expedition to North Holland, before again commanding a brigade in the Mediterranean.

Upon his return to Britain he was appointed lieutenant governor of Jamaica (1805-1808), and then second in command to Lord Chatham in the Walcheren expedition. Although the siege of Flushing under his direction ended in success, he conducted it in a manner which suggested he could no longer be trusted with command. His career ended in dishonour when in 1816 he was dismissed for conduct unbecoming to an officer and a gentleman (it seemingly involved flagellation and boys from Christ's Hospital School).

The **1st Foot**, popularly known at this time as the Royals, later the Royal Scots, was the senior regiment of the line, founded in 1635 and known as Pontius Pilate's Bodyguard. The first battalion went to the West Indies with Craddock in 1790 and was then transferred to St Domingue where in two years it lost five officers and 400 men to disease, mainly yellow fever. The second battalion, meanwhile, had been posted to serve as marines, and saw action at Toulon (1793) and Corsica (1794). The battalion continued to serve in the Mediterranean until called upon to join the expedition to North Holland. Like the Guards it experienced the landings at Callantsoog under Abercromby's command, and like the Guards it was commended for its soldierly appearance by Moore, in whose brigade it served. The battalion then became part of Pulteney's force at Ferrol, before joining Abercromby at Gibraltar. Obviously having impressed the commander-in-chief, it became part of the Army of Egypt.

The first battalion of the **54th Foot** (West Norfolk) was known to Abercromby, both from its service in Flanders (1794-1795) and then when it was under his direct command during the brief campaign to suppress a rising in St Vincent (1796). The second battalion was raised in 1800 and the ranks were filled with militia volunteers. Both battalions took part in the aborted Ferrol expedition before joining Abercromby at Gibraltar.

Major General Eyre Coote.
(Author's Collection)

The **92nd Foot** (Gordon Highlanders) was raised only in 1794 by the 5th Duke of Gordon in response to the threat posed by the French Revolutionaries. This made it one of the youngest regiments of the line. After a brief period on Corsica, and then Elba, the regiment served in the garrison at Gibraltar. Returning to Europe in 1798, it was involved in the suppression of the Irish Rebellion, and then joined the expedition to North Holland. Even before the troops had the chance to prove themselves in action, Moore described them as an outstanding unit, and they soon lived up to his praise, including making a quick recovery from the chaos at Callantsoog. In 1800 they were intended for the attack on Belle Île but when this was abandoned they sailed for Minorca, apart from a small detachment that had been armed with rifles and was undergoing light infantry training. These were with General Sir James Pulteney's force for the proposed attack on Ferrol, and like the 54th they joined Abercromby at Gibraltar.

1st Foot: blue facings, paired lace, double blue
54th Foot: popinjay green facings, lace paired, green
92nd Foot: yellow facings, lace paired with blue stripes, a kilted regiment
Total strength as of 7 March: 2,129 (626 + 974 + 529)

The 2nd Brigade

Major General Sir John Cradock (1759-1839), son of the Archbishop of Dublin, was yet another of Abercromby's Irish brigadiers. He joined the 4th Regiment of Horse in 1777 and then transferred to the Coldstream Guards two years later. His subsequent regiments were the 12th Light Dragoons (major) and the 13th Foot, of which he became lieutenant colonel in 1789. He was with them in the West Indies in 1790, where he returned in 1793 with Grey's expedition, eventually becoming the general's aide de camp. He was appointed major general in 1798, when he was also made quartermaster general in Ireland. He took part in the suppression of the Rebellion, and was with Cornwallis in the defeat of the French invasion that followed. In 1801 he was posted to the Mediterranean and given a brigade command in Abercromby's expeditionary force.

He was later commander-in-chief in Madras, followed by command of the British forces in Portugal (1808-1809). After a brief period in Gibraltar he was appointed governor of Cape Colony (1811). This proved to be his final official position.

8th Foot (King's) served in Flanders and was praised for an audacious night attack on French lines at Nijmegen in 1794. The regiment became part of the garrison of Minorca in June 1799, the island having been taken from the Spanish at the end of the previous year. The 8th was one of the battalions that sufficiently impressed Abercromby to be detached from garrison service and replaced by a less effective unit.

The **13th Foot** (1st Somersetshire), like the 1/1st, were sent to the West Indies with Cradock in 1790 against the threat of a French attack on British interests. In 1793 they and the Royal Scots were transferred to St Domingue

(French Haiti) to aid French settlers against the uprisings of mulattos and free blacks. By 1795 their strength was so reduced that the men were drafted into other regiments and the officers and NCOs were sent back to Britain to recruit. Brought up to strength, they were involved in the suppression of the Irish Rebellion before forming part of Pulteney's abortive Ferrol expedition. They then joined Abercromby at Gibraltar and took part in the similarly aborted expedition to Cadiz.

In 1793 the **18th Foot** (Royal Irish) were sent to Toulon from garrison duty in Gibraltar in a failed attempt to aid the Royalists who had risen against the Revolutionaries' take-over of power. They then took part in the successful campaign to eject the French from Corsica. When Britain decided to leave Corsica in 1796, the 18th were evacuated to Elba. They then returned to Gibraltar, where they joined Abercromby's force in 1800.

The **90th Foot** (Perthshire Volunteers), like the 92nd, was privately raised in 1794 by a leading Perthshire landowner, Sir Thomas Graham, who was himself a volunteer. It was trained as a light infantry battalion and was sent to Quiberon Bay in 1795 in what proved a failed attempt to support the rebels against the Revolutionary government in the Vendée. It was also part of the force under Sir Charles Stuart that took Minorca in 1798, and remained there in garrison before being integrated into Abercromby's force.

8th Foot: blue facings, blue and yellow lace
13th Foot: yellow facings, paired yellow lace
18th Foot: blue facings, paired blue lace
90th Foot: buff facings, paired lace, alternate blue and buff striped, Tarleton helmet
Total strength as of 7 March: 2,138 (439 + 561 + 411 + 727)

The 3rd Brigade

Major General Richard Lambert, 7th Earl of Cavan (1763-1837) was the fourth of the expedition's Irish brigadiers. He succeeded to his father's title in 1778 and the following year was commissioned into the Coldstream Guards, rising to first major by 1800, although he had already been placed on the general list in 1798. Like Ludlow, he served with the Coldstreamers in Flanders, being wounded at the siege of Valenciennes, and later with Pulteney at Ferrol. He then joined Abercromby at Gibraltar. In August 1801, he took command of the Guards Brigade when Ludlow transferred to a line brigade. At the successful conclusion of the campaign he remained in Egypt in command of both Hely-Hutchinson's and Baird's troops that had been left to hold the country against any renewed French attack.

All his subsequent service was home based.

The **50th Foot** (West Kent) became known as the *Blind Half Hundred* after the Egypt campaign because they suffered so severely from ophthalmia. Earlier in the French Revolutionary Wars they had been involved in the defence of Toulon in support of the Royalists and in the ejection of the French from Corsica. After a period of garrison duty in Gibraltar they were sent to Portugal in 1797, remaining there for two years, after which they joined the garrison on Minorca and were selected by Abercromby for his Mediterranean force.

The **79th Foot** (Cameron Volunteers) was another Scottish regiment raised by a powerful landowner, in this case Sir Alan Cameron of Erracht, who drew on men from his own clan when the French declared war on Britain. The regiment first saw active service in Flanders in 1794, and performed well in the defence of Nijmegen. This was followed by two years on Martinique, which seems to have been a royal response to Sir Alan's refusal to disband his regiment after the collapse of the First Coalition. Warned by the Duke of York that the king would send it to the West Indies, Sir Alan is supposed to have retorted that the king could send it to Hell if he chose but he, Sir Alan, would lead it there. In 1799 it was involved in the North Holland campaign and experienced the mismanaged landings at Callantsoog. Having also been part of Pulteney's force that failed at Ferrol, the regiment then joined the army of Egypt at Gibraltar.

The oldest English line regiment, the **2nd Foot** (Queen's) had detachments in the West Indies and serving as marines at the outbreak of the war with France. The marines were with the Channel Fleet and served with Howe at the first British victory of the war, The Glorious First of June. The marines were then sent to join the rest of the regiment in the West Indies and took part in Grey's conquest of Guadaloupe (1794). Three years later they were with Abercromby at Trinidad and Puerto Rico. They then served in Ireland during the rebellion before forming part of Abercromby's advance force in North Holland. Like the 89th they experienced the confusion of the landings. They were then sent to Belle Île in 1800, and when this expedition was abandoned because the defences were thought to be too strong, they spent an extended period at sea before they arrived in Malta, where they joined Abercromby's expeditionary force, originally as part of Doyle's Brigade. They transferred to the third brigade to replace the invalided 27th (see below).

50th Foot: black facings, paired red lace
79th Foot: dark green facings, paired lace, one yellow and two red; a kilted regiment
2nd Foot: blue facings, regular blue lace
Total strength: 1,611 (477 + 604 + 530) [including 2nd]

The remaining two battalions of the brigade were the **1/27th** and **2/27th** (Inniskilling) but they were so weakened by sickness that the first battalion was left on Malta, the second battalion having already been sent to Lisbon. The second battalion recovered so quickly, however, that it arrived in Egypt just in time for the landings. The Inniskillings were well known to Abercromby, having served under his command in the West Indies, where they played a notable part in the conquest of St Lucia, and in North Holland.

27th Foot: pale buff facings, regular blue and yellow lace

The 4th Brigade

Colonel John Doyle (1756-1834), yet another Irishman, was commissioned into the 48th Foot in 1771 and then transferred to the 40th with which regiment he fought in North America. Although he only had the rank of lieutenant, he was actively involved in raising the 105th, the Volunteers of Ireland, with his friend, Lord Rawdon, later 2nd Earl of Moira. He returned to North America with the new regiment and saw more action against the Colonists. The 105th was disbanded in 1784 but at the outbreak of war nine years later Doyle set about raising yet another Irish regiment, the 87th (Prince of Wales' Irish), of which he was appointed lieutenant colonel. He fought with them in Flanders under Moira's command and was part of Moira's expedition to Quiberon Bay (1795). Upon his return to Ireland he was appointed Irish Secretary at War but then resigned to serve in the Mediterranean, taking up a staff position at Gibraltar before going on to Minorca, having volunteered to serve with Abercromby.

Egypt was his last period of active service, although he was later placed on the general list and also proved an active and effective lieutenant governor of Guernsey.

The **30th Foot** (Cambridgeshire), known as the *Old Three Tens*, saw action as marines at Toulon and Corsica, and at the Battle of Cape St Vincent. Although the regiment was in Ireland during the rebellion, it did not become involved in the subsequent brutal suppression. It was then sent to the Mediterranean, and was posted on Sicily before being transferred to Malta where it was part of the blockading force under Thomas Graham. The men of the 30th earned particular approbation from Abercromby when he inspected them on Malta, and were chosen to join the army of Egypt in place of the ailing 1/27th and the two-battalion 40th, the ranks of which were full of Europe-only militia volunteers.

The centre companies of the **44th Foot** (East Essex), *The Fighting Fours*, served in Flanders (1794), and were with Abercromby at Boxtel, while the flank companies were in the West Indies with Grey (Martinique, St Lucia and Guadeloupe). The whole regiment served with Abercromby when St Lucia was re-taken (1796). After a short period of home service it was sent to the Mediterranean to serve with the Gibraltar garrison, from where it sailed to Malta to join the Army of Egypt.

The **89th Foot** was another volunteer regiment raised in 1793 in response to the French threat, in this instance by Lieutenant Colonel William Crosbie in Dublin. It joined York's army in Flanders in 1794 and was later posted to Ireland, where it took part in the suppression of the Irish Rebellion. This won the regiment the nickname *Blayney's Bloodhounds* in recognition of the determination with which Lord Blaney, lieutenant colonel of the regiment, hunted down rebels. In 1800 the 89th joined the 30th on Malta for the blockade of Valetta and, like the 30th, was chosen by Abercromby to replace the battalions that could not serve in Egypt.

> 30th Foot: pale yellow facings, bastion shaped lace, one wide sky blue stripe
> 44th Foot: yellow facings, regular blue yellow and black lace

89th Foot: black facings, paired red and blue lace

Total strength: 1,053 (412 + 263 + 378)

The 5th (Foreign) Brigade

Brigadier General John Stuart (1759-1815) was an American Loyalist who had been educated in England. He was commissioned into the 3rd Foot Guards in 1778 and served with them in North America. He was with Cornwallis at the surrender of Yorktown. After the outbreak of war with France he went with the Guards to Flanders, serving directly under Abercromby's command at various actions and during the difficult winter retreat of 1794-1795. He was appointed to command a brigade under Sir Charles Stuart, serving with him in Portugal in 1797 and during the capture of Minorca the following year.

Promoted to major general in 1802, he subsequently commanded a brigade that was posted in east Kent against the threat of French invasion. He then accompanied General Sir James Craig to the Mediterranean. He spent some time in Gibraltar and Malta before moving on to Sicily (1806), which had been invaded by the French. On 4 July 1806 he successfully attacked General Reynier's force at Maida. Although this victory was not followed up, it demonstrated the point made in Egypt, that British troops could challenge the French in battle and win. He continued to operate in the Mediterranean, taking the island of Ischia in 1809. After a brief period as lieutenant general of Grenada, he was appointed to a home command at Plymouth but soon resigned on the grounds of ill health.

The Minorca Regiment was raised on Minorca by General Sir Charles Stuart. Part of the defending force on the island was a Swiss regiment in Spanish service made up of Germans, Austrians, and some Hungarians. They had been taken prisoner in Italy by the French in 1796 and sold on to the Spanish at two dollars a man. After the British had taken the island they willingly transferred to British service, suggesting the flexibility of the more pragmatic soldiers of the day. After Egypt, they were taken into the line as the 97th Foot (Queen's Own Germans).

De Roll's Regiment was founded by Baron Louis de Roll, a captain in the Swiss Guard who survived the massacre at the Tuileries Palace in August 1782. At the end of 1794, after he had served in Flanders with the Comte d'Artois, de Roll recruited for a two-battalion regiment of Swiss, many of them formerly in the Guard, although numbers were later augmented by recruits from Alsace and the German states. The new regiment, never numerous enough to justify two battalions, entered British service and was sent initially to Corsica. When that island was evacuated, the troops went on to Elba. The regiment was next in Portugal, in 1797, where Sir Charles Stuart had been entrusted with the defence of Lisbon. By this time it had the title, Royal Foreigners. It took part in the capture of Minorca (1798) after which it became part of the British garrison on the island. Abercromby had used foreign units in the West Indies, and seems to have had no problem with accepting them into his Egypt force.

Dillon's Regiment was raised in North Italy in 1795 by Edward Dillon, who had served in the Irish Brigade of the old French Royalist army. Most of the officers were French émigrés, while the men were predominantly French and Italian. The regiment first served on Corsica, before being transferred to Elba and then, like de Roll's, joined Sir Charles Stuart's force in Portugal. It took part in the conquest of Minorca before becoming part of the garrison.

> Total strength: 1987 (929 + 528 + 530)
> Minorca Regiment: yellow facings, regular black lace
> De Roll's Regiment: light blue facings, regular blue lace, black, broad-brimmed hats
> Dillon's Regiment: yellow facings, bastion-shaped regular dark grey lace, round hats or shakos

The Reserve

This, the largest brigade, was commanded by **Major General Moore** (see above), with **Brigadier General Hildebrand Oakes** (1754-1822) as second-in-command. Oakes was commissioned into the 33rd Foot in 1767 and served with them in North America under Cornwallis. He transferred to the 66th Foot with the rank of major, rising to lieutenant colonel in 1795, at which point he transferred to the 26th Foot. He was aide de camp to Sir Charles Stuart on Corsica, and was also appointed deputy quartermaster general (1794). Still with Stuart, he served as quartermaster general in Portugal (1797). He accompanied Stuart to Minorca, when it was taken from the Spanish.

After Egypt he held various other staff positions: at Portsmouth and in the South West, in the Mediterranean, and as governor of Malta. His final staff position was Lieutenant General of the Ordnance (1814-1822).

The **23rd Foot** (Royal Welsh Fusiliers) went to the West Indies in 1794 with Grey's expedition but were then transferred to St Domingue, where the Fusiliers took part in the capture of Port-au-Prince. They returned to Britain in1796, like most regiments that served in the Caribbean their numbers decimated by the effects of climate and disease. They then had to find recruits from the unsatisfactory manpower available. They were involved in the expedition to North Holland in 1799 before being sent to Île de Houart, preparatory of the attack on Belle Île in 1800. When this expedition was aborted, they sailed to Minorca, becoming part of Abercromby's force.

The **28th Foot** (North Gloucestershire), popularly known as *The Slashers*, served in Flanders throughout the campaign that ended with the winter retreat to Bremen (1793-1795). The regiment was then sent to the West Indies in 1795, although a detachment of four companies was stationed in Gibraltar, where the remnants of the West Indian companies joined them in 1797. The following year the regiment took part in the capture of Minorca, where they then remained as part of the garrison.

The **42nd Foot** (The Black Watch) was also involved in the Flanders campaign, arriving with Lord Moira as part of the force intended for action at Quiberon Bay. These troops remained in the Netherlands after Moira's departure and were with Abercromby at Boxtel. Five companies went with Abercromby to the West Indies, while the other five were sent to Gibraltar. The West Indies detachment served on St Lucia and then St Vincent, where it helped suppress a French-inspired uprising. The detachment returned to the Caribbean in 1797 as part of Abercromby's force that took Trinidad but failed at Puerto Rico. Back in Europe, after it had been brought up to strength, the detachment then joined the Gibraltar companies and subsequently became part of Stuart's Minorca expedition.

The **58th Foot** (Rutlandshire) was another of the regiments that accompanied Grey to the West Indies and took part in the capture of Martinique and Guadeloupe. It then saw action in Stuart's capture of Minorca.

The two-battalion **40th Foot** (2nd Somersetshire) served in the Netherlands towards the end of the Flanders campaign before the flank companies went to the West Indies with Grey. The flank companies returned to Britain with Grey but the whole regiment was then sent back to the Caribbean, serving first on St Vincent and then transferring to San Domingue. When it came back to Britain for the second time, early in 1799, it was seriously understrength and took in large numbers of Europe-only militia volunteers to fill the ranks (Major Jackson in his journal gives a vivid picture of the desperate efforts to introduce some sort of order before the troops set sail). Following service in North Holland, the regiment spent a brief period in Ireland, before being sent to Minorca. Abercromby intended to leave it on Malta because of the large number of Europe-only volunteers but the men themselves were so eager to serve in Egypt that he relented and took the four flank companies with him.

The **Corsican Rangers** was originally formed of Corsicans and French émigrés who fled with the patriot leader, Pasquali Paoli, after Britain abandoned the island. They took the title *Franc Tireler Corse*. They were officially recognised and taken into British service in November 1799 under the command of Major Hudson Lowe, but did not adopt the title Corsican Rangers until after the landings at Aboukir. On Abercromby's order, they were armed with Baker rifles.

> 23rd Foot: blue facings, bastion shaped regular red blue and yellow lace
> 28th Foot: yellow facings, paired lace, 1 yellow, two black
> 42nd Foot: blue facings, bastion shaped regular red lace, a kilted regiment
> 58th Foot: black facings, regular red lace
> 40th Foot: deep buff facings, paired black and red lace
> Corsican Rangers: black facings, green jackets, sky blue breeches
> Total strength: 2,726 (457 + 587 + 754 + 469 + 250 +209)

Cavalry Brigade

Major General the Hon. Edward Finch (1756-1843) was commissioned into the 11th Dragoons in 1778, then served briefly with the 20th Light Dragoons before transferring to the 87th Foot. He went with the regiment to the West Indies and North America. He next joined the Coldstream Guards as lieutenant and captain and served with them in Flanders as captain and lieutenant colonel. He was involved in the suppression of the Irish Rebellion in 1798 and commanded the first battalion of the Coldstreamers in North Holland a year later. In 1800 he was appointed to command of a cavalry brigade which formed part of the Army of Egypt. During the campaign he transferred to a line brigade.

He subsequently commanded the 1st Brigade of Guards at Copenhagen (1807). This was his last active service because his seniority to Wellington prevented him from serving in the Peninsula.

The **11th Light Dragoons** became a light cavalry regiment in 1785. Two squadrons fought in Flanders, particularly distinguishing themselves at Le Cateau on 26 April 1794, and at Tournai two weeks later. After four years of home service they returned to the Low Countries in 1799 as part of the Anglo-Russian expedition to North Holland. Only the two troops of C Squadron were sent to Minorca and thus became part of the Army of Egypt.

The **12th Light Dragoons** (Prince of Wales') became a light cavalry regiment in 1768, when the 12th Dragoons were restyled the 12th (Prince of Wales) Light Dragoons. A squadron was involved in the capture of Corsica in 1794, and the whole regiment was briefly in Italy before returning to Britain for a period of home service in 1795. It was then sent to Portugal in 1797, as part of Sir Charles Stuart's force intended for the defence of Lisbon against a possible Spanish attack (the Spanish being allies of France). Late in 1800 they were sent to Marmaris Bay to become part of the expeditionary force to Egypt. Unfortunately, at this stage the men were without their horses, and even when some were supplied by the Turks they proved undersized and fewer than had been promised.

The **26th Light Dragoons** were embodied in 1795 in Jamaica, remaining in the West Indies until 1797. They returned to Britain, only to be sent to Lisbon, like the 12th, as part of a defensive force. Again like the 12th, they arrived at Marmaris Bay late in 1800, and joined Abercromby's expedition.

Hompesch's Light Dragoons (Hussars) should more accurately be described as Hompesch's Mounted Riflemen. They were originally attached to Hompesch's Fusiliers, raised by Baron Charles Hompesch and his brother. In1798 they became a separate corps, and sailed to Ireland, where they acted with the 5/60th, also predominantly German, in the suppression of the rebellion. They then joined Pulteney as part of the expedition to Ferrol, and were absorbed into Abercromby's force after that expedition was aborted.

> 11th Light Dragoons: buff facings, white lace, Tarleton helmet
> 12th Light Dragoons: pale yellow facings, white lace, Tarleton helmet
> 26th Light Dragoons: blue facings: white lace, Tarleton helmet
> Hompesch's Light Dragoons (Mounted Rifles): red facings, green jacket,
>   red breeches

Artillery

Brigadier General Robert Lawton R.A. (1741/2-1816) began his military career in 1758 as a cadet at the Royal Military Academy, Woolwich. He first saw action at Belle Île in 1761 as lieutenant-fireworker. Following promotion to first lieutenant, he was with Cornwallis in North America, where he was appointed bridgemaster in 1779. By 1793 he was Major Lawton R.A. and had set up the first troop of Horse Artillery, the Chestnut Troop. In 1800 he was appointed brigadier general in command of the artillery attached to Abercromby's army.

He was confined to home service after his return from Europe, particularly home defence against the threat of a French invasion. In 1808 he was placed on the general list.

The 13th, 14th, 26th, 28th, 55th, 69th, 70th, and 71st companies of the Royal Artillery served in Egypt, totalling 759 officers, NCOs and other ranks. Their field pieces comprised 24 light 6-pounders, four light and 12 medium 12-pounders, and six howitzers. For siege work they had four 12-pounders, two ten-inch and 10 eight-inch howitzers, and 36 mortars of various sizes.

Royal Artillery: red collar and cuffs, white turn backs, bastion-shaped yellow lace (blue jacket)

There was also a small contingent of Royal Engineers, all officers as was the whole corps. They wore blue, tailed coats with black collars, cuffs and lapels.

Reinforcements

In order to eject the French from Egypt it would be necessary to take both Cairo and Alexandria, initially attacking one while blockading the other. This would require more troops than Hely-Hutchinson, succeeding to command after Abercromby's death, had at his disposal. He sent an urgent request to London for reinforcements, which finally arrived in July and August. Hely-Hutchinson then reorganised his force, creating a sixth brigade to which Lieutenant Colonel John Blake (1762-1836) of the newly arrived 24th Foot was appointed with the local rank of brigadier general.

The **20th Foot** (East Devonshire) had been part of the force sent to North Holland in 1799. They were sent to Minorca, where they were one of the regiments Abercromby chose to leave on the island because of the large number of militia volunteers in the ranks. When the call for reinforcements arrived, however, they volunteered for service in Egypt, arriving on the 18 July two battalions strong. Although they joined the campaign so late, the men of the 20th were among the worst sufferers from ophthlamia.

Pale yellow facings, red and black lace

The **24th Foot** (2nd Warwickshire) served in Canada from 1789 until 1800, with the specific task of protecting the border from American incursions.

The battalion was a late addition to the force the Duke of York scraped together in England for service in Egypt, where they arrived on the 14 July.

Blue-green facings, paired wide green and narrow red lace

The **25th Foot** (Sussex) served as marines at the outbreak of the Revolutionary Wars. Detachments were on ships in the Mediterranean, the English Channel and the North Sea, and the flank companies were with Howe at the Glorious First of June (1794). A second battalion, raised in 1795, was sent to the West Indies to help suppress the uprising on Grenada. The 25th also saw action during the expedition to North Holland (1799). Like the 24th, they were one of the regiments York selected for service in Egypt, in their case because their ranks were filled with beyond-Europe men.

Yellow facings, blue-yellow-red lace

The **26th Foot** (Cameronians) were sent to Canada in 1787 and remained there until 1800, when they sailed back to England. Like the 25th, although their numbers had been made up with volunteers from the militia, these were men who were prepared to serve beyond Europe. They arrived in Egypt in mid-July.

Pale yellow facings, paired yellow-blue-yellow lace.

The Ancient Irish Fencibles had been raised in Dublin in 1799. Like all Fencible regiments, they were raised locally against a specific threat, in this case a French invasion. The Ancient Irish volunteered for service abroad and were sent to Minorca, where they arrived little better than a rabble. A period of training, however, meant that Abercromby could use them to release a regular unit from garrison duty. Despite the restriction on their serving outside Europe, they were chosen to reinforce the army in Africa, much to the indignation of the men in the ranks. When Africa proved to be Egypt, however, attitudes changed and, landing on the 18 July, the men proudly proclaimed that they were all volunteers now.
It is impossible to be certain about uniform. It was in the British style but it seems that jackets of various lengths and different types of headgear were worn, suggesting a rather *ad hoc* method of equipping the unit. One certain fact, however, is that the buttons bore the Irish harp.

There were also three foreign regiments in the reinforcements.
The **Chasseurs Britanniques** had a new name but actually comprised troops from foreign regiments in the French Royal Army, Swiss, German and Irish, who had fled at the outbreak of the Revolution, and responded to the Prince of Condé's call for troops. From 1794 they were paid by the British, although they operated with the Austrians, and later with the Russians. The Tsar's defection from the Second Coalition brought them back to the Austrians until the Peace of Lunéville (February 1801) took Austria out of the war and led to the disbandment of Condé's force. About 700 men refused to give up the fight and were taken into British service. They were immediately sent to Egypt.

Their uniform comprised green jackets with half lapels and grey breeches. Yellow facings, no lace. Their equipment was black, from their Russian service.

De Watteville's was another of the units in British pay which initially fought with the Austrians. Its antecedents were the four émigré regiments formed in March 1798, after the French invasion of Switzerland. Like Condé's troops, the Peace of Lunéville brought an end to joint action with the Austrians. Baron Frederic de Watteville united the remnants of the four regiments, augmented with some of Condé's men, and brought them into British service. They were sent to Malta, along with the Chasseurs Britanniques, before sailing on to Egypt, where they arrived on the 3 August.

The regiment was issued with uniforms from a British supply depot. They wore green jackets with black facings and light blue pantaloons.

Löwenstein's Jägers (also known as Rifles or Light Infantry) were embodied in 1800 when Prince Löwenstein-Wertheim signed an agreement with Britain to raise a corps of riflemen for British service (his third, following chasseurs and fusiliers). By the end of the year the corps was nearly 500 strong, mainly Bavarians. They originally operated with the Bavarian army in conjunction with the Austrians but once Austria was out of the war those who did not desert were transported by British ships from Trieste to Malta. After a brief spell on Elba, they were shipped to Egypt and saw some action in the final stages of the campaign.

Their uniform comprised blue grey jackets with green half lapels, cuffs, collars and turn backs, blue grey breeches and Austrian jäger hats.

The only cavalry troops York could find were the **22nd Light Dragoons**, raised in 1794 and yet to see service. Unfortunately, there were no horse transports available but they arrived in Egypt on the 24 July where they served as a dismounted unit.

In addition to these reinforcements, Hely-Hutchinson also received a detachment from the 3rd Foot Guards, 300 men strong, and 120 gunners from Gibraltar.

Summary

To sum up, it can be seen from the above summaries that all the infantry and cavalry units that formed the Army of Egypt had some recent military experience. Unfortunately, *some experience* is an appropriate description. There had been no great victories on land of which the nation could boast. Such success as had been achieved did not suggest that any British army would ever be able to meet the best of the French armies with even some slight hope of holding its own. And the French Army of the Orient was crowned not only with their victories in Egypt and Syria but also with the laurels of Napoleon's first Italian campaign of 1796. Even the British seizure of islands in the Caribbean, probably the army's most notable achievement, had been against troops of a very different quality from those that now awaited them, and, despite some success, Grey's and Abercromby's campaigns, as well as events on St Domingue, had revealed the rawness of the British troops.

Yet, whether in the West Indies, in the conquest of the islands of Corsica and Malta, even in the debacle of the Flanders campaign, something positive in the British soldier's make-up was apparent. Although he did not cope well when circumstances were stacked against him, ask him to stand and he would stand without protest. Give him the scent of victory and he would pursue it relentlessly. Abercromby was well acquainted with these qualities, and would hope to exploit them in Egypt.

Perhaps the most significant of the campaigns of the 1790s was the expedition to North Holland in the autumn of 1799. It is notable how many of the troops from that campaign, now present in the Army of Egypt, had been with Abercromby at the initial landings and in the subsequent actions, particularly the Battle of Egmont (also known as the Battle of Alkmaar). That expedition ultimately failed for a variety of reasons for which the troops were not to blame: the difficulty of working with an unpredictable ally, the inefficiencies and failures of government provision for the campaign, and the over-optimistic expectations of the foreign secretary, whose brainchild the expedition was, to name just three. However, the actual conduct of the army gave promise of something better; something very much better, as Abercromby himself acknowledged. If only the troops were properly trained and equipped, disciplined, cared for, and given a realistic objective, there was a chance of success. Everything would depend upon preparation.

The Indian Contingent

At this point it is important to take a look at Baird's army. Although their role would essentially be of a secondary nature, they were still vital to the overall plan. The French needed to anticipate an attack from the Red Sea, and take measures against it, to enable Abercromby's main attack to succeed.

Major General Baird brought three infantry battalions from India, plus a contingent of native soldiers in the service of the East India Company, comprising 1,200 Bengal sepoys and two battalions from Bombay. This was the first time sepoys had been used on foreign service: it was assumed that they would cope better with the harsh climate. Once this force had landed on the Red Sea coast, it was augmented by a further British infantry battalion and a troop of the 8th Light Dragoons from the Cape of Good Hope. For guns Baird had some horse artillery from the Cape and a detachment of East India Company artillery.

The **10th Foot** (North Lincoln) had seen no active service in the first years of the war. The regiment was sent to India in 1798 and was initially stationed at Madras before being sent to the Bengal Presidency. The expedition to Egypt promised the regiment its first active service since the American War.

The **61st Foot** (South Gloucestershire) joined Baird's force from the Cape, where the regiment had been sent in 1799. At the outbreak of the war it had been in garrison at Gibraltar. The following year it sailed to the West Indies with Grey – Henry Dundas recognised that troops stationed in Gibraltar developed some immunity to the endemic diseases of the Caribbean. The regiment was involved in operations on Martinique and St Lucia, and also served under Abercromby in 1796 during the second conquest of St Lucia. In October of that year, however, the surviving men were sent back to Britain, where the regiment focused on replenishing the ranks. In 1797 it was sent to Guernsey, before sailing to the Cape two years later.

The remaining battalions in Baird's force were all raised in 1793 in response to the French declaration of war. The **80th Foot** (the Staffordshire Volunteers) mainly comprised men from the Staffordshire Militia, most of whom came from the estates of Lord Uxbridge, the man who raised the regiment. They were sent to Guernsey before they had received any training beyond that given to them by the militia. They were then sent on to Flanders as part of Lord Moira's force but succumbed almost immediately to an outbreak of yellow fever which originated from their being crammed into un-fumigated transports. As a result they remained in the Low Countries until the end of the campaign instead of accompanying Moira to the Vendée. Once they had been evacuated from North Germany, however, they were sent to take the Île d'Yeu, in support of the French Royalists. They finally returned to Britain in 1796, now only at half-strength. Later in the same year they were sent to the Cape of Good Hope and then on to Ceylon, recently taken from the Dutch, where they remained until called up for Egypt.

The **86th Foot** (the Shropshire Volunteers) was raised by an American Loyalist, Sir Cornelius Cuyler, whose wife had family connections in Shropshire. It was originally intended as a volunteer unit, but in 1794 the regiment became part of the British Army Establishment. Sent to Ireland in the same year, the men were then transferred to serve as marines. In 1796 they were reunited from their various ships and posted to the Cape of Good Hope to serve in garrison. Three years later they transferred to India, serving in the Bombay Presidency, although three companies were detached to Ceylon.

The third of the relatively new regiments was the **88th Foot** (Connaught Rangers), raised in Ireland by the Honourable Thomas de Burgh from men on the estates of his father, the Earl of Clanricard. Like the 80th, the 88th was sent to Flanders with Lord Moira in 1794, although as a result of a storm only two companies actually arrived. The rest went on to Gibraltar, from where they were transferred to the West Indies. They formed part of Abercromby's force in 1795 and saw action on Grenada, but like all the regiments posted to the Caribbean they then needed to return to Britain to make good their losses. They sailed to India in 1799, arriving in Bombay in June 1800, from where they were transferred to Ceylon to join an expedition intended for an attack on Dutch-held Java. Instead, they were redirected to join Baird's expedition to Egypt.

10th Foot: bright yellow facings, regular blue lace
61st Foot: buff facings, regular blue lace, round hat
80th Foot: yellow facings, paired lace two red, one black
86th Foot: yellow facings, paired lace, two yellow, two black
88th Foot: pale yellow facings, paired lace, two black, two red, one yellow

A single troop of the **8th Light Dragoons** (King's Royal Irish) was Baird's only cavalry. The regiment had been in Flanders in 1794, and was sent to the Cape in 1796. Like the 61st, it joined the Indian contingent at Suez.

8th Light Dragoons: red facings, white lace (light grey jacket, tropical helmet)

1st Bombay Native Infantry: yellow facings, red jacket with yellow collar, cuffs and lapels, white turnbacks

7th Bombay Native Infantry: yellow facings, regular white lace, red jacket with yellow collar, cuffs and lapels, white turnbacks

Bengal Volunteers: no details

Madras Artillery: blue jacket, red cuffs and lapels, white turnbacks

For a full order of battle and unit strengths, see Appendix II.

It might be surmised that this was something of a hotch-potch force, but no more so then Abercromby's Army of Egypt, which had come together more by chance than design. That had been the norm since 1793. Together, though, the two forces presented the first realistic British threat to French military hegemony.

The Naval Contingent

The Commander of the Mediterranean Fleet was **Admiral George Elphinstone, Lord Keith** (1746-1823). Abercromby was famed for his ability to work harmoniously with senior naval officers – not always the easiest of tasks – as he had proved in the West Indies and North Holland campaigns. Yet there is evidence to suggest that Keith proved the exception. After the failure at Cadiz, Abercromby wrote a letter to an undersecretary at the Admiralty, which found its way to Lord Spencer, First Lord of the Admiralty. In this letter the general expressed his fear that he could not rely on Keith, and implied that he would welcome a change of command in the Mediterranean. For reasons of protocol, this was not possible, but the fact that Abercromby expressed such reservations about Keith did not bode well for conjunct operations in Egypt. It also raises the question: what was it about Keith that aroused such serious doubts in a man who was well-known for his equable temper and his firm belief that there should be no friction between senior naval and army officers?

Elphinstone, as he then was, entered that navy as a midshipman in 1761, serving on HMS *Royal Sovereign* before transferring to serve under Captain John Jervis on HMS *Gosport*. As he progressed in rank he acquired a reputation for greed. Certainly, he was acquisitive, which he proved while attached to the East India Company. Having borrowed £2,000, he concentrated on trading ventures that made him a fortune, to which he then assiduously added. By 1775 he had reached the rank of post captain. In the American War he made a name for himself by sweeping up the privateers who operated off the east coast and seizing the ships of both the colonists and their European allies. He was also in command of a naval brigade at Charleston. In other words, he was a talented sailor, but a man whose weakness was cupidity.

At the end of the American War, though, he found himself without a ship, so he dedicated himself to a political career, which certainly did no harm to his financial situation. The outbreak of war with France brought him back into action. He was at Toulon under Admiral Hood in 1793. Two years later, as a rear admiral, he was instrumental in the capture of the Cape of Good Hope, and he also played a prominent part in restoring order after the mutiny at the Nore in 1797. This was the point at which he received his Irish title. In 1798 he was second-in-command to Jervis at the Battle of Cape St Vincent and the following year he was appointed to the Mediterranean command. His first task was to support the Austrians at the siege of Genoa, but Marengo soon made cooperation pointless. Then came the expedition that caused Abercromby to write his letter. The plan was to destroy the Spanish fleet at Cadiz, which required the navy to land the army and then remain offshore ready for re-embarkation. Keith, who seems to have been ignorant of conditions in the waters around Cadiz and only discovered how potentially perilous they were once he was there, refused to commit himself on the viability of the landings, no matter how strongly Abercromby urged him to give an opinion. This confirmed for Abercromby Keith's reputation as a man who made sure that someone else would take the blame if things went wrong – while at the same time insisting on his share of any prize money.

Second in command of the naval contingent was **Rear Admiral Sir Richard Bickerton** (1759-1832). He was the son of a vice admiral and his father exploited the system to enter the young Richard into the service in 1771. The boy drew his pay, although he could not actually serve until 1774. He was posted to HMS *Medway* as captain's servant, but soon rose to midshipman and lieutenant. After a period in command of the sloop HMS *Swallow*, on convoy duty in the channel where he had the opportunity to display considerable enterprise, he joined Admiral Rodney in the West Indies and took part in the conquest of Sint Eustatius in 1781. As post captain in command of HMS *Invincible* he was also present at the Battle of Fort Royal in the same year. He went on to operate in the Leeward Islands and in North American waters but, like Keith, he was on the beach once the war ended. He succeeded to his father's baronetcy in 1792, when war with France was imminent. The following year he joined the Channel Fleet before being transferred back to the West Indies. By 1799 he was with the Mediterranean Fleet with his flag in HMS *Seahorse*, having been promoted to rear admiral. He brought Abercromby, Hely-Hutchinson, and Moore to Minorca in *Seahorse*, and established a better relationship with them than was possible with Keith. At Cadiz Bickerton was one of the senior naval officers most frustrated by Keith's vacillation.

Another officer who felt the same way as Bickerton, and shared his feelings with John Moore, was **Captain Alexander Cochrane** (1758-1832), son of the Earl of Dundonald (and uncle of Thomas Cochrane). He joined the navy as a boy and served during the American War. By 1778 he had the rank of lieutenant. Like Bickerton, he served with Rodney in the West Indies as a signals officer. Again like Bickerton, he gained experience in command of a sloop, HMS *St Lucia*. In 1782 he was promoted to post captain, but at the end of the war he suffered from the inevitable government cutbacks. In 1790, though, when there seemed a very real possibility of war with Spain over the incident at Nookta Sound, he was given command of a frigate. In the first year of the French war he took eight French privateers while in command of HMS *Thetis,* and then continued these attacks in North American waters. Transferring to HMS *Ajax* in 1799, he was involved in the subsequently abandoned expeditions to Belle Île and Ferrol. He was then attached to the Mediterranean Fleet under Keith. As a result of Cochrane's ability to work with the army, as demonstrated at Cadiz when he established an immediate rapport with Abercromby, he was chosen to work with Anstruther on the preparations for the landings in Egypt.

Captain Sir William Sidney Smith (1764-1840), always known as Sir Sidney Smith, might best be described as a flamboyant maverick. He came from a family with strong naval traditions, so it is no surprise that he joined the navy at thirteen. He served in the American War and in 1780 was promoted lieutenant under Rodney for excellent conduct, even though he was under age. He attracted even more attention at the Battles of Cheasapeake Bay (1781) and the Saintes (1782), after which he was given command of the sloop, HMS *Fury*. Before the end of war he had been promoted to captain, but like so many naval officers he then found himself on the beach. He used the time to visit France, Spain and Morocco, taking the opportunity to involve himself in intelligence activities for which his mind was well suited. In 1790 he was given permission to serve with the Swedish navy in their war with Russia and was subsequently knighted by the Swedish king. Somewhat surprisingly, George III permitted him to use the title.

In 1792, when the Prussians and Austrians launched their first attacks on Revolutionary France, Smith was in Turkey but he immediately returned to Europe and went to Toulon, where he destroyed a large number of French ships during the final evacuation, although not enough to satisfy Admiral Hood. He then served with the Western Frigate Squadron in command of HMS *Diamond*. He demonstrated his initiative by setting up a naval battery on Île Saint-Marcouf, which was held until the Peace of Amiens. At the same time, he was being viewed with increasing suspicion by his fellow naval officers, and with distaste by the French. Consequently, when he was taken prisoner while operating off the French coast, he was held at the Temple prison for two years, intermittently under sentence of death, and only escaped with Royalist help. In 1800, after Nelson's victory at Aboukir, Smith was sent to the Mediterranean in command of HMS *Tigre*. There was a diplomatic dimension to this posting, which he exploited by sailing to Acre in support of the Turks. The city was under siege by Bonaparte, and Smith's involvement proved crucial to the French failure to take it. Still in his diplomatic guise, he tried to negotiate a peace between the Turks and *Général de Division* Kléber, in command after Bonaparte's departure to Paris and power. This was a step too far and Keith nullified the agreement. He could not prevent Smith becoming involved in Abercromby's expedition, however, because Smith's useful links to the Turks and knowledge both of the Egyptian coast and of French resources made him an invaluable source of information.

The fleet brought to Aboukir Bay by Keith comprised seven ships of the line, five frigates, and twelve armed corvettes, as well as two bomb ketches.

5

The Campaign

Setting the Scene

When Bonaparte departed for France, he left the Army of the Orient under the command of *Général de Division* Jean-Baptiste Kléber, a talented commander and a man of considerable intellectual power who would have proved a difficult opponent for the British. After Kléber's assassination by a Muslim fanatic in June 1800 command passed to *Général de Division* Jacques Menou, an able administrator but far less impressive as a field commander, and much given to voluptuary pleasures. The tragedy of Kléber's death was one of those unforeseen factors that can have a crucial influence on subsequent events.

The French held Alexandria and Cairo as their main strongholds, while detachments guarded the Red Sea ports. Menou was in Cairo, while *Général de Division* Friant commanded at Alexandria with 5,000 men. Although the coast was under British naval blockade, the French were confidently expecting reinforcements to be brought from France by *Contre-Amiral* Honoré Gantheaume.

As already discussed, the strategy conceived by Henry Dundas required inter-service cooperation, and an alliance with the Ottoman Turks. The main force under Abercromby was to secure possession of Alexandria before marching to Cairo. A second force, raised in India, was to sail for the Red Sea ports and then march to Cairo to link up with Abercromby. The defeated French would be given passage back to France. The saving grace of this strategy, again as noted, was its clear objective: to remove the French from Egypt.

Dundas had devised a scheme for the conduct of the campaign based on the facts as he understood them. Because of his close relationship with Abercromby, however, and his trust in his friend's judgement, he granted him a freer hand than generals had previously enjoyed during the war. As he wrote:

> I do not mean to exclude your judgement, if the result of further enquiry should lead you to form a decided opinion contrary to the instructions you have received. From the naval advice you have with you, and the various channels of information which the Mediterranean affords, it is not impossible you may receive such

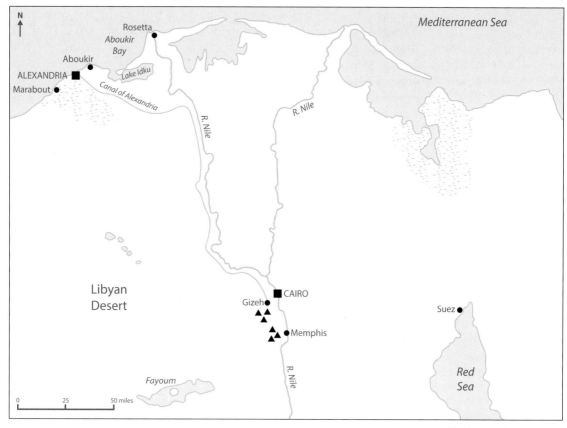

The theatre of operations.

information and intelligence, either with respect to the navigation to Egypt, or with regard to the circumstances in which that country now is, as may induce either in whole or in part to postpone the execution of the service committed to your charge, and I shall not repine at whatever exercise of that discretion may be. In your hands I feel the interests of the country safe in this respect.[1]

Abercromby certainly had reservations about the enterprise but, like Dundas, he recognised that if the French were ejected from Egypt Bonaparte would lose one of his strongest cards. He believed that Europe stood on the brink of an honourable peace, and possession of Egypt would help bring the negotiations to a satisfactory conclusion. For this reason, at the age of 66, he was prepared to fight one last campaign for king and country.

The following timeline includes the main events and relevant details of the campaign. Some actions (as indicated in the text) are subsequently considered in more detail.

24 October 1800

Having finally received orders from England, Abercromby and Pulteney, who were at Gibraltar, reorganised their forces so that the majority remained

---

1   Dunfermline, *Abercromby*, p.251.

with the former while the later took the corps with the highest proportion of limited service men. Pulteney was to proceed to the defence of Portugal. Those with Abercromby accepted that their service would take them beyond Europe. Why else would the weak 44nd Foot take the place of the much stronger 63rd except that the ranks of the latter were full of men not for general service? The assumption, which proved justified, was that they were about to embark for Egypt.

27 October
Colonel Anstruther, quartermaster general, and Lieutenant Colonel Murray sailed to Rhodes to open communications with the Turks. On the same day, the first division sailed for Minorca but soon afterwards contrary orders instructed only those ships in need of serious repair to head to Port Mahon. The remainder were to make for Malta.

5 November
All the ships destined for Malta had now set sail. Between 400 and 500 sick had to be left behind in Gibraltar, while the 2/27th, seriously affected by fever, was sent to Lisbon. The following weeks were stormy, however, so that for some of the fleet the voyage was protracted.

26 November
Although Abercromby and Keith reached Malta on the 19 November, some of the fleet were yet to arrive, including those that were under repair at Minorca. While he waited for them Abercromby inspected the island's defences and sent Dundas his opinion that in the event of peace Britain should claim Malta because it was of more strategic value than Minorca. He also embodied a corps of Maltese Pioneers who were attached to the staff corps.

20 December
The First Division, under Abercromby, sailed for Marmaris Bay, arriving on the 29 December. The Second Division, under Hely-Hutchinson, set sail a few days later and arrived on the 1 January. During an enforced stay of six weeks careful preparations were made for the forthcoming campaign (see Chapter 3).

11 January 1801
The horses which had been purchased by order of Lord Elgin, the British ambassador in Constantinople, arrived but proved to be too small and badly galled to be of any use. Instead, parties were sent into the countryside to buy the small but spirited local horses.

14 January
Rear Admiral Sir Richard Bickerton and Sir Sidney Smith, who had been cruising off Alexandria, now arrived at Marmaris.

23 January

Major General Moore arrived from Jaffa with the dispiriting news that the Grand Vizier had no plans for immediate action and that his army was completely disorganised. Thus, any landing on the Egyptian coast would depend entirely on British resources.

17 February

At an assembly of all the general officers and the senior naval officers, Abercromby explained his intentions and gave his final instructions. News also arrived that two French frigates had been able to elude the naval blockade, which was dispersed by a storm, and put into Alexandria. They brought much needed ammunition, and 800 gunners.

22 February

Embarkation began on the 18 February, but took four days to complete. At 7:00 a.m. the signal to release mooring ropes was given from Keith's flagship, the *Foudroyant*. This was followed by the signal for weighing anchor. At 5:00 p.m. Bickerton gave the signal that all the ships were clear of the harbour.

25-27 February

The progress of the fleet was hampered by severe weather conditions. The waves were mountainous and even the largest ships laboured against them, while the smaller vessels, the gunboats and the feluccas, sought shelter in the lee of the island of Cyprus.

1 March

Land was finally sighted. The weather still being capricious, the fleet stood off all night. Another French frigate reached Alexandria, landing 200 men of the 51e Demi-Brigade, six hundred gunners and yet more ammunition, while a brig brought intelligence that Gantheaume, who was known to be heading for Alexandria, had with him 5,000 reinforcements.

2 March

The British ships now entered Aboukir Bay and signals were made for landing. Then the wind freshened again, the surf ran high, and the signals had to be cancelled.

News arrived of the death of Major McKerras, the senior engineer. He and Major Fletcher R.E. had been reconnoitring ashore some days before but as they were returning to the sloop HMS *Peterel* they were chased by a French gunboat. McKerras was hit by a lucky shot and died instantly and Fletcher was taken prisoner. This was a blow beyond the personal response to McKerras's death because R.E. officers were few in number and the expedition would feel the loss of these two.

3 March

Abercromby and Moore took a schooner close inshore to reconnoitre the coast ready for the landings. They realised that the only feasible landing point was towards a range of low dunes dominated by a much steeper sand hill. To the right the troops would come within range of the guns of Aboukir Castle; to the left, there was a blockhouse, also armed with guns.

6 March

Sir Sidney Smith went inshore with two armed launches to deal with a gunboat which was stationed at the entrance to Lake Maadieh (Lake Aboukir), whereupon the French abandoned the boat, dismantling the vessel after they had thrown its gun into the lake. Sir Sidney brought back with him a French corporal of artillery who informed Abercromby that the force preparing to contest the landings was 2-3,000 strong.

7 March

In response to the information from the French corporal, Abercromby sent Moore and Colonel Lindenthal, an Austrian serving with the British army, inshore to reconnoitre the preparations the French had made against the landings. Although the weather was initially boisterous, conditions then moderated and it was decided that the landings should be attempted the following day, according to the routine practised at Marmaris.

8 March

The landings finally took place, and succeeded in copybook fashion. Despite strong French resistance, by early afternoon the beach and the dunes that lay beyond were in British hands (see Chapter 6).

9 March

Although adverse winds prevented the landing of stores and provisions, the troops did at least find a fair supply of good water when they dug about four feet into the sand. They were also able to fashion some kind of shelter out of the boughs of the date trees, a privation Abercromby shared with his men. There was also some reorganisation of the disposition of the troops. Men from Stuart's and Doyle's brigades who had originally been sent to Aboukir Castle were replaced by the 2nd (Queen's) and Hompesch's dismounted dragoons, whose horses had not yet been landed. Also, the 2/27th arrived from Lisbon, strong enough now to re-join the expedition.

Abercromby instructed Moore and Anstruther to check the ground for a suitable forward position. They had with them the 92nd, the Corsican Rangers, and some cavalry. When they came up against some French cavalry, they withdrew slightly and took position near an old redoubt and a flagstaff. They decided that, with the sea on one side and Lake Maadieh on the other, this narrow neck of land represented a good position to hold ground. When this fact was reported to Abercromby, he ordered Moore to occupy it with the reserve.

10 March

It was now possible to land the horses by making use of Lake Maadieh, which was proving navigable for small craft although soundings were still being taken. The lake also offered a good supply of fish and, if uniformly deep enough, a safe haven for the naval gunboats. Indeed, the lake was to prove of vital significance to the conduct of the campaign.

A detachment of the Corsican Rangers under Lieutenant Guittera was pushed forward by Moore to persuade a weak detachment of French cavalry to withdraw. Unfortunately, they advanced too close to a French redoubt at Mandorah and were surrounded by enemy cavalry. The officer, the surgeon, and thirteen men were taken prisoner.

Général de Division Lanusse had now arrived from Cairo with 5,000 men.

11 March

A flag of truce was sent into Aboukir Castle inviting the commandant to surrender but he refused.

Abercromby joined Moore to assess the forward position and also to explain that only the problem of landing sufficient stores had delayed the advance of the rest of the army. Now that Lake Maadieh had proved to be deep enough for small craft, this difficulty no longer existed.

12 March

The army commenced a march in two columns at 7:00 a.m. to join up with the forward troops. There was some resistance from French cavalry of the 22e Chasseurs à Cheval posted near some Roman ruins which the French called Caesar's Camp, but after some smart skirmishing the advance of the British infantry caused the French to withdraw. By 1.30 a.m. the troops were in their new positions, in two lines extending from the sea to Lake Maadieh. The French were posted on a range of hills ahead of them and held a strong position. They opened up their batteries on the British, which resulted in two men killed and two wounded, but the French guns were then silenced by some return of fire. The troops remained under arms all night and the 90th and 92nd were posted as advanced picquets.

13 March

A second encounter with the French, at Mandorah, aimed to turn the enemy's right. It led to fierce fighting which resulted in the British occupying their opponents' position and the French withdrawing to a position under the walls of Alexandria (see Chapter 6).

14 March

Abercromby now set about fortifying this new position. The heavy guns and more ammunition were landed which meant that the investment of Aboukir Castle could commence.

15 March

The first tents and other camp equipage were issued. The local Arabs also arrived with the offer of fresh food. During the night of the 14 March Colonel Brice of the Coldstreamers lost his way in the dark and was killed when he strayed too close to the French while inspecting the forward posts.

There were also several attempts by the French to drive in the British vedettes, which served little purpose and cost them some casualties. Abercromby wrote to Friant that it would be better to reduce the inevitable calamities of war by resisting the temptation to engage in activities that risked men lives without benefiting the general cause. Friant wrote in reply that he agreed, and the attacks stopped.

17 March
A part of the garrison of the castle launched a sortie against the works the British had been building ready for a regular siege and nearly succeeded in overwhelming the fifty marines manning them. The 2nd (Queen's) intervened in time to drive the French back.

18 March
Aboukir Castle surrendered and the 2nd (Queen's) re-joined the main army, to be replaced by a battalion of marines, 500 strong.

The 12th and 26th Light Dragoons engaged in a pointless charge against a strong French cavalry patrol which had concealed infantry support. They took heavy casualties when they came under French artillery fire. A general order was issued instructing the troops to be under arms thirty minutes before daybreak on a daily basis.

19 March
In a general order Abercromby castigated the cavalry for their recklessness the previous day. The 92nd, which had suffered heavily at Mandorah, was ordered to Aboukir Castle, as a replacement for the marines.

The first Turkish detachment arrived, comprising about 500 troops from the secondary force, while a further 5-6,000 were hourly expected. The first view of their allies did not inspire much confidence.

Abercromby confided to Moore that he saw their position as extremely challenging but he believed they were committed and would have to attack the French for a third time. For the same reason he also prevented Keith from sailing away from Aboukir Bay to go in search of Gantheaume. Yet at the same time he admitted that he risked throwing away a fine army. In other words his was a situation that no-one would envy.

20 March
At noon Menou arrived in Alexandria from Cairo with 9,000 troops. He immediately gave orders for an attack on the British, to take place before daybreak the following day.

21 March
Menou planned to drive the British into Lake Maadieh and then harry them back to their ships. In this third encounter, however, the British troops displayed the discipline and steadiness of conduct that would become so apparent in the Napoleonic Wars (see Chapter 6). General Abercromby was wounded during the action.

23 March
A flag of truce was sent into Alexandria inviting the French to surrender, with the promise that they would be transported back to France, and could take everything with them except their artillery and the shipping currently in the

harbour. Menou sent a scornful response to this offer of what he described as ignoble terms.

25 March

The Captain Pacha, High Admiral of the Ottoman Empire and in command of the secondary force, and the most competent Turkish commander, anchored in Aboukir Bay. He had five ships of the line and 3,600 troops, Turks and Albanians. These were in addition to the 500 who had already arrived. Furthermore, over a thousand of the new troops were reputed to have been trained by the Pacha to a high standard. The Grand Vizier, however, had yet to cross the Sinai Desert, although he was known to have left Jaffa on the 25 February and was reported to be on the Egyptian side of the border.

The French, now blockaded in Alexandria, were again invited to surrender. Menou refused.

28 March

Lieutenant General Abercromby died aboard Admiral Keith's flagship, HMS *Foudroyant*. A musket ball had lodged in his thigh bone, close to the hip, and extraction proved impossible. He died of sepsis. Major General John Hely-Hutchinson now succeeded to command of the campaign. Being little known and with some unattractive qualities of character, he was viewed with considerable suspicion by officers and men alike. He was also essentially a theoretical soldier and spent some days deciding how to continue the campaign. One possibility was a concerted effort to take Alexandria, for which purpose the senior naval officers suggested cutting the banks of the canal in order to flood Lake Mareotis to a depth of ten feet. This would allow their gunboats to get close to the city, which would effectively be cut off. It would also facilitate the regular arrival of stores. Alternatively a secondary attack could be launched against Damietta, which would allow joint action with the Vizier when he finally arrived.

2 April

The Captain Pasha inspected the British troops but seemed unimpressed by their plain uniforms and the marks of their recent hard fighting. Several French deserted from Alexandria, including a mameluke who received a generous gift from the Captain Pacha.

Hely-Hutchinson finally decided that it would be advantageous to take Rosetta, possession of which would open up the Nile and the more fertile land it flowed through. Colonel Brent Spencer was ordered to march there with the 58th, the four flank companies of the 40th, which was his own regiment, Hompesch's Light Dragoons, who had been remounted, and three guns. This detachment was accompanied by 4,000 Turkish troops, commanded by the Captain Pacha.

3 April

For the first time the troops felt the effects of the khamsin, which was to blow intermittently for the next few months and was blamed for the increasing incidence of ophthalmia.

6 April

Having been delayed by severe weather at Aboukir, Spencer now continued his advance, reinforced by the 2nd (Queen's).

Major General David Baird, in command of a force which was drawn from different parts of India and Ceylon, set sail from Bombay for the Red Sea with about 3,000 men.

8 April

Spencer's detachment reached Elko, about fourteen miles from Rosetta. The small town had been evacuated by a party of French cavalry the previous day, but only after an orgy of plundering. Because of the conditions there, the troops spent the night two miles further on.

9 April

Hely-Hutchinson was still considering an attack on Alexandria. Colonel Cameron of the 79th was sent with a detachment of 200 men to reconnoitre the canal and reported back that there was no opposition.

Spencer's force arrived within three miles of Rosetta, after a difficult march through sand hills. Rosetta had also been abandoned by the French, who had hurriedly crossed the Nile when news of the British advance reached them. They had left a garrison, mainly of veterans, in Fort Julien, which meant that the allied troops had to march another two miles in order to form line before the fort.

On Hely-Hutchinson's order, Spencer sent the Hompesch Dragoons back to Aboukir. The French had been issuing inducements to persuade them to desert, and three men had taken up the offer. The remainder, about 200 strong, were deprived of their horses and posted at Aboukir Castle.

10 April

The 2/1st (Royals) were sent to reinforce Spencer's detachment.

13 April

The 18th and 90th also marched to join Spencer. Hely-Hutchinson ordered the flooding of Lake Mareotis by cutting the dyke of the canal of Alexandria at seven points. For the watching troops, the tumultuous onrush of water was a peculiarly satisfying sight but the force of the water united four of the cuts into a single gap which was too wide to be bridged. In order to maintain communications boats were stationed near the opening. They were also used to ferry the Arabs and their supplies to the British position.

14 April

Colonel Spencer ordered the 2nd (Queen's), under Colonel Lord Dalhousie's command, and supported by a thousand Turks, to besiege Fort Julien. He had been awaiting not only the heavy guns, which had to be dragged across desert and swamp, but also seven British and Turkish gunboats, which also had to be dragged for several miles across difficult ground in order to avoid some French gunboats which guarded the mouth of the river. Once launched, the allied boats forced the French boats to take refuge under the walls of the fort. This enabled yet more allied boats onto the river, whereupon the French boats were quickly disposed of.

17-18 April
The allied batteries now opened fire on Fort Julien. The 17th and 30th reached Rosetta and were followed by the 8th and 79th, under the command of Major General Cradock, who superseded Spencer, and Brigadier General Doyle.

19 April
The garrison holding Fort Julien surrendered on the same terms as the garrison at Aboukir Castle. The British and Turks now had unopposed passage along the banks of the western branch of the Nile, accompanied by support boats. It was now possible to advance on Ramanieh, which was vital to French communications.

20 April
Rear Admiral Sir John Borlase Warren joined Keith off Alexandria with seven ships of the line, having dispersed Gantheaume's fleet as it sailed to relieve the French.

22 April
News arrived at headquarters that Rear Admiral John Blankett had arrived at Suez with 600 troops, while others were expected to arrive in the near future. This was Hely-Hutchinson's first information on Baird's whereabouts.

24 April
Hely-Hutchinson, preceded by Anstruther, left the camp to take command of Spencer's troops who were now posted at El Hamad, bringing with him the 50th and the 92nd. He had already decided to attack a body of French troops under *Général de Brigade* Lagrange, who were entrenched at the village of El Aft. During Hely-Hutchinson's absence Major General Coote took command of the remaining 6,000 troops, who were preparing to blockade Alexandria.

25 April
Because navigation across the Red Sea was difficult and there were few maps to guide the ships, Baird's fleet was obliged to separate into smaller contingents, which were then further dispersed by storms. Consequently, when Baird reached Mocha he discovered that part of his fleet had sailed on to Jeddah after a brief stay at Mocha, rather than to the agreed rendezvous of Kosseir (Quseir).

28 April
Once more of his troops had reached Mocha, Baird sailed with them to Jeddah, where he arrived on 18 May, only to discover that the ships he had expected to find there had sailed on to Suez.

1 May

Osman Bey, who had recently succeeded to command of the Mamelukes in Upper Egypt (his predecessor, Mourad Bey, having been an ally of the French), offered his services to Hely-Hutchinson in return for British protection from the Turks. This was felt to be a welcome development because the Mamelukes were disciplined cavalry who knew the country and were highly respected by the local inhabitants.

5 May

Hely-Hutchinson advanced his force in two columns towards Ramanieh, the right under Cradock along the shore of Lake Edko and the left, under Doyle, marching along the banks of the Nile. They took up a position to the north of the village of Derout, while the Turks were posted about two miles ahead of them. Colonel William Stewart of the 89th had been detached the previous day to cross the Nile with his own battalion, plus 20 men from the 12th Light Dragoons, an artillery detachment, and 1,200 Albanians from the Captain Pacha's force, these being the best-trained of the Turkish forces. By this move Hely-Hutchinson hoped to prevent the French from troubling the British flank or interfering with the progress of the 50 British and Turkish gunboats that were supporting the advance.

7 May

During the night of the 6th the French withdraw from their strongly fortified position at El Aft, which allowed the British to occupy it the following day. The French had carried everything away with them, although thirteen germes, the traditional Nile boats, carrying rice and stores were intercepted. Five Frenchmen were unfortunate enough to fall into the hands of some Albanians, who decapitated them and brought the heads back so that they could claim the customary monetary reward from their commanders.

Meanwhile, Coote was anxious to set up a line of communication with Hely-Hutchinson using cavalry patrols but he lacked sufficient horses, whereupon the officers of his brigade offered their own horses.

8 May

Major Moore, 26th Light Dragoons, commanded a detachment of 100 dragoons which was ferried across the Nile during the night of the 7 May and advanced as far as Birket, but failed to find Hely-Hutchinson's patrols.

Hely-Hutchinson now knew that a French force comprising 3,000 infantry and 800 cavalry, was holding a strong position at Ramanieh behind the canal of Alexandria. The cavalry was on the right, close to the Nile, while the left was protected by four guns mounted on a low fort.

9 May

At 5:00 a.m. Colonel Stewart and his detachment began an advance to Disuq, where they were to attack the French. An hour later Stewart became aware that a small party of French cavalry appeared to be reconnoitring his strength, which at this time consisted only of the British troops because the Turks had yet to come up. The French then sent out about 300 or 400 men, all arms, to cut Stewart off. He formed up the 89th, depending on the gunboats for further protection, but the arrival of the Albanians distracted the attention of the French and Lord Blaney was able to advance the 89th to prevent the French retreating to their boats. They immediately came under fire from the French but Stewart ordered the British guns to open up, which enabled the 89th to get behind the enemy. The result was a sharp struggle, with the French finally managing to reach their boats and make their escape across the river. Each side lost a gunboat but the British seized seventy-three germes loaded with supplies.

At the same time Hely Hutchinson marched on Ramanieh itself. At about midday he halted when he realised that the French cavalry was drawn up in line of battle. He then advanced in two lines, the first comprising the Turks on the left and Cradock's brigade on the right, and the second, the Reserve under Spencer on the left and Doyle's brigade on the right. British cavalry was in front of the Turks, with Turkish cavalry to their left. The latter were able to check the effectiveness of the French skirmishers as the British force advanced, although a French gun eventually caused them to lose all order. The Turkish infantry, however, continued their forward movement despite the attention of the enemy skirmishers. The right reached the canal of Alexandria, which the French had now abandoned, and remained there until the light started to fade. At this point the Turks came under strong French attack and Cradock's and Doyle's brigades had to move to the left to cover their retreat. The light companies then saw off the French advance, whereupon the whole French force drew back.

The first of the Vizier's troops reached Damietta, which forced the French to abandon their stronghold at Lesbeh, thus losing command of the Damietta branch of the Nile. The French troops would subsequently become prisoners on board British and Turkish ships as they struggled to make their way by sea to Alexandria.

10 May

Général de Brigade Lagrange abandoned Ramanieh during the night and marched his troops in the direction of Cairo. This meant that French communications between Cairo and Alexandria had effectively been severed. The 100 men whom the French had left in the fort, along with some sick, surrendered. Taking Ramanieh was a mixed blessing, however, because it soon became apparent that the plague had been raging there. Hely-Hutchinson posted sentinels at all access points to keep the British soldiers out, and the place was subsequently garrisoned by the Turks. It was also the point where Hely-Hutchinson found himself faced by what can only be described as a potential mutiny, not from the men but from the senior officers. He had given orders for a further advance the following day, but this was opposed seemingly by all his generals and their immediate subordinates. Nor were they tactful when voicing their disagreement. Hely-Hutchinson stood firm, however, and the march took place the following day as he intended. Interestingly, Major Robert Wilson, who was serving with the Hompesch Dragoons, wrote in his journal that, although it was a risky undertaking to advance towards Cairo without any idea of what lay ahead, such was the quality of this new British army that they might be judged capable of anything.

A fleet of twenty store ships and victuallers reached Aboukir Bay from Britain. They also conveyed the 1/27th, about 500 strong, who had previously been left to recover from an outbreak of sickness, as well as about 500 recruits and convalescents who belonged to various battalions. On Hely-Hutchinson's orders, the 1/27th marched to Rosetta under the command of Colonel Thomas Graham.

11 May

As a concession to the conditions, Hely-Hutchinson decided that the men's knapsacks should be transported by boat, which was confirmed by a general order of 13 May. This did not prevent his officers continuing to voice their protests against advancing into the unknown in the hottest season of the year. In fact, Hely-Hutchinson had suffered a loss of nerve, perhaps in response to the opposition he was facing, and decided to return to Rosetta. His plan, therefore, was not to advance as far as Cairo, but to pursue Lagrange long enough to drive him back to that city so that he would not be able to attack the Vizier. He also intended that the Vizier should withdraw to Salahieh, out of reach of Lagrange. Unfortunately, he kept this information to himself, sharing it only with Moore, who was at Rosetta, still recovering from the wound he received on 21 March. The mutineers, for they can be described as nothing less, conceived a plan to deprive Hely-Hutchinson of command and actually wrote to Moore and Coote for their approval.

The army continued to advance as previously, with Stewart on the far bank of the Nile, and marched about twelve miles to Shubra.

12 May

The army advanced to Kafr Houdig, and remained there the following day because the boats had not caught up. The waters of the Nile were falling and the boats were also hindered by the khamsin. On a more positive note, there was news of the imminent arrival of reinforcement: about 1,200 from Malta, and the first certain news that the force from India had reached Jeddah, while Rear Admiral Blankett's contingent was now at Suez. They would need camels in order to cross the desert, but the camels were with the Vizier, who now needed to remain at Bilbeis. At the same time, there could be no return to Rosetta. Hely-Hutchinson knew that he needed to advance much closer to Cairo in order to protect the Turks and wait for Baird's force.

14 May

The army reached the villages of Kafr Laheis and Shabur, while Stewart took up a parallel position on the other bank of the Nile. During the day a flotilla of French germes, loaded with ammunition, uniforms, and about £5,000, was taken by the Turks. The convoy had set sailed from Cairo, heading for Ramanieh before news of events there had reached the city. The boats were guarded by about 200 men of the 25e Demi-Brigade. They came ashore as soon as the Turks attacked, and fought desperately in order to avoid what they knew would be their fate if they fell into Turkish hands. Fortuitously for

'Bonaparte leaving Egypt'; contemporary British caricature. The departure of Bonaparte and several of his key subordinates helped open the way for British intervention in Egypt. (Author's Collection)

A French view of the evacuation of the British army from Den Helder in 1799. The lessons of this ultimately-failed campaign would be applied to good effect when Abercromby planned the landings in Egypt. (Author's Collection)

The landings at Aboukir Bay, viewed from the fleet. (Author's Collection)

The landings at Aboukir Bay – aquatint by Sutherland. (Author's Collection)

The death of Abercromby – aquatint by Sutherland. (Author's Collection)

Private of the 30th Foot during the Egyptian campaign as depicted by Henri Boisselier. (Collection of Yves Martin)

Officer of the 11th Light Dragoons during the Egyptian campaign as depicted by Henri Boisselier. (Collection of Yves Martin)

Above left: Private of 11th Light Dragoons, carrying guidon. This figure shows the basic light dragoon uniform, with Tarleton helmet and short blue jacket decorated by lace. (Anne S.K. Brown Military Collection)

Above right: Officer of 12th Light Dragoons wearing the ornate mirliton-style headdress adopted by officers of this regiment. (Anne S.K. Brown Military Collection)

Left: Officer of the 22nd Light Dragoons, showing the more typical appearance of light cavalry officers at this time, albeit with non-regulation blue breeches. (Anne S.K. Brown Military Collection)

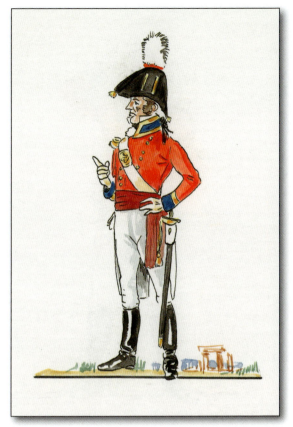

Above left: Coldstream Guards officer. Always being well equipped, the Guards regiments were distinguished from one and other by the arrangement of lacing and buttons – in this case, paired: all wore the blue facings of a royal regiment. (Anne S.K. Brown Military Collection)

Above right: Coldstream Guards light company officer. Note the light infantry 'wings' on the shoulders. (Anne S.K. Brown Military Collection)

Right: 2/1st Foot, Ensign with Regimental Colour. (Anne S.K. Brown Military Collection)

Above left: 2nd Foot, Sergeant. This illustrates the basic line infantry uniform as outlined in Appendix I, with the ordinary arrangement of lace. NCO distinctions include the chevrons, sash, and halberd. (Anne S.K. Brown Military Collection)

Above right: 23rd Fusiliers, Officer. The 23rd was the only one of the Army's three fusilier regiments to take part in this campaign: it is doubtful that the bearskin fusilier cap was worn on day-to-day service, for reasons which this illustration make apparent! (Anne S.K. Brown Military Collection)

Left: 26th Foot, Drummer. Drummers' uniforms were inevitable ornate, and based on reversed colours so that the coat was the colour of the regiment's facings. (Anne S.K. Brown Military Collection)

Above left: 28th Foot, Private. A rear view, showing pared-down accoutrements as worn for battle. Note the queued hair. (Anne S.K. Brown Military Collection)

Above right: 50th Foot, Officer. Broad-brimmed hats were widely adopted due to the hot climate. (Anne S.K. Brown Military Collection)

Right: 90th Foot, Private. Raised by Sir Thomas Graham as light infantry unit, the 90th adopted a crested helmet in lieu of the shako. (Anne S.K. Brown Military Collection)

Above left: 42nd Highlanders, Piper. The senior of the three Highland regiments to serve in Egypt, the 42nd wore Government sett tartan and the blue facings of a Royal regiment. (Anne S.K. Brown Military Collection)

Above right: 79th Highlanders, Officer. Note the sash worn over the shoulder, and the broadsword. (Anne S.K. Brown Military Collection)

Left: 92nd Highlanders, Corporal. This is the standard rank and file Highland uniform, marked only by the rank chevrons on the sleeve. (Anne S.K. Brown Military Collection)

Above left: Stuart's Minorca Regiment, Private. This depiction shows Anton Lutz with the standard captured from the 21e Légère at the battle of Alexandria. In most respects, this regiment was uniformed much as British line units. (Anne S.K. Brown Military Collection)

Above right: De Roll's Regiment, Officer. This figure shows another variant on officers' headwear; the rank and file wore broad-brimmed hats. (Anne S.K. Brown Military Collection)

Right: Dillon's Regiment, Private. Again, dress is much like that of the British line infantry; note the bastioned lace, a design also worn by the 23rd, 30th, and 42nd amongst the 'Egyptian' regiments. (Anne S.K. Brown Military Collection)

Above left: Corsican Rangers, Private. Although having similarities with the British Army's new rifle battalions, the tight laced breeches are a decidedly continental touch. (Anne S.K. Brown Military Collection)

Above right: Löwenstein's Jägers, Private. The uniform echoes that of the Austrian *jäger* regiments, reflecting this unit's continental origins. (Anne S.K. Brown Military Collection)

Left: Hompesch's Light Dragoons (Hussars), Private. Again, the dress of this corps reflects its continental origins. (Anne S.K. Brown Military Collection)

Above left: Bombay Native Infantry, Sepoy. This was the traditional uniform of sepoys, as used by both the British and the French since middle of the 18th century – sandals on feet or barefoot. (Anne S.K. Brown Military Collection)

Above right: 8th Light Dragoons, Private. The only mounted troops with Baird's Indian contingent, the 8th wore the tropical version of light cavalry uniform with light grey jacket. (Anne S.K. Brown Military Collection)

Right: 8th Light Dragoons, Officer. A variant on the rank and file uniform, retaining the light grey jacket but with the more familiar Tarelton helmet. (Anne S.K. Brown Military Collection)

Above left: 10th Foot, Sergeant. The senior line infantry regiment with Baird's contingent, showing yet another variant on headgear. (Anne S.K. Brown Military Collection)

Above right: 86th Foot, Colonel. The officer depicted here would seem to be Lieutenant Colonel Robert Bell, who succeeded to command the regiment in January 1801 and retired in 1802. (Anne S.K. Brown Military Collection)

Left: 88th Foot, Private. Another rear view, this time in full marching order for the long trek across the Nubian Desert. The harp on the backpack cover is an interesting detail. (Anne S.K. Brown Military Collection)

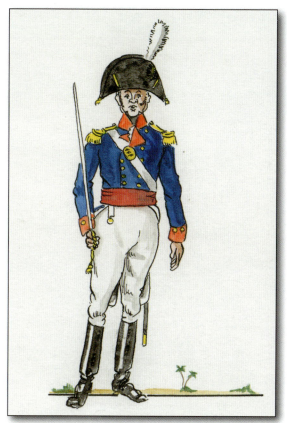

Above left: Royal Artillery, Officer. As part of the Ordnance rather than the Army, jackets were blue. (Anne S.K. Brown Military Collection)

Above right: Royal Artillery, Private. Official headgear was the bicorne, but some preferred the previously worn 'Mother Shipton' hat which was less cumbersome. (Anne S.K. Brown Military Collection)

Right: Marine, Corporal. Marines followed the conventions of the regular army, but the uniforms were provided by the Navy Board – this led to a time-lag in supply and many were therefore still wearing the open style jacket. Upon return from Egypt they became the Royal Marines, so facing changed from white to blue to signify a Royal regiment. (Anne S.K. Brown Military Collection)

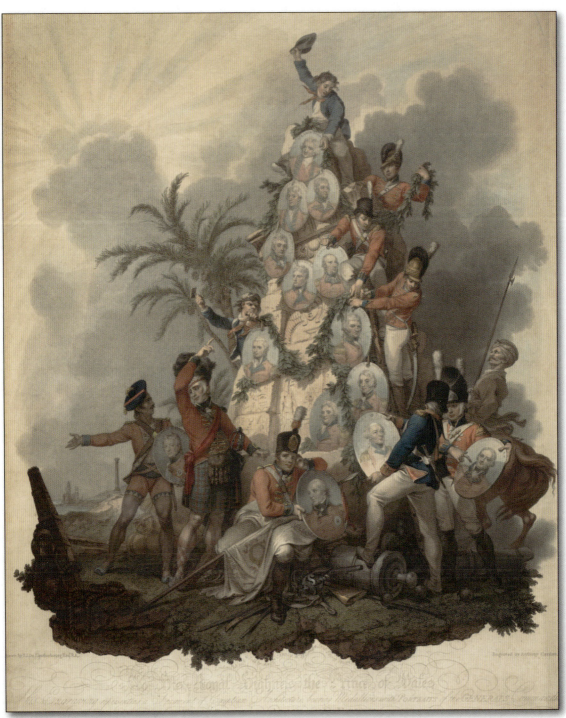

'Fragment of Egyptian architecture bearing medallions with portraits of the generals commanding the British Army in Egypt and otherwise illustrative of the ever memorable conquest of that country'. (Philip James de Loutherbourg, 1806). (Anne S.K. Brown Military Collection)

them, a reconnoitring party of the 11th Light Dragoons arrived in the nick of time and the French were able to surrender to a more civilised opponent. The French dead and those too seriously wounded to walk were decapitated in the usual Turkish fashion, however. Doyle was detached with the cavalry and a battalion from his brigade to pursue some French who had been seen marching towards Damanhur, but by the time he arrived, there was no sign of them.

16 May

Hely-Hutchinson reached Algam. Major Wilson, who had been sent to the Vizier, returned with the disturbing news that he had been unable to dissuade him from attacking a French force advancing from Cairo. Hely-Hutchinson expected the worst, a crushing Turkish defeat which would take them out of the war. He had to wait several days before news of the outcome reached him.

As already noted, the Vizier had left Jaffa on 25 February and advanced slowly, hindered by bad roads. He also lost large numbers to the plague. By 15 March he was at Gaza and two weeks later at El Arisch. He was making his way towards Cairo and his approach forced the French garrisons at Salahieh and Belbeis to abandon their posts and withdraw to Cairo. Detachments had also occupied Damietta and Lesbeh. He finally paused at Belbeis on 11 May in the expectation that *Général de Division* Belliard, in command at Cairo, would march against him in order to drive him back into the desert before the British arrived. On 30 May the Vizier sent Major Hope R.A., part of the

Hely-Hutchinson's advance on Cairo.

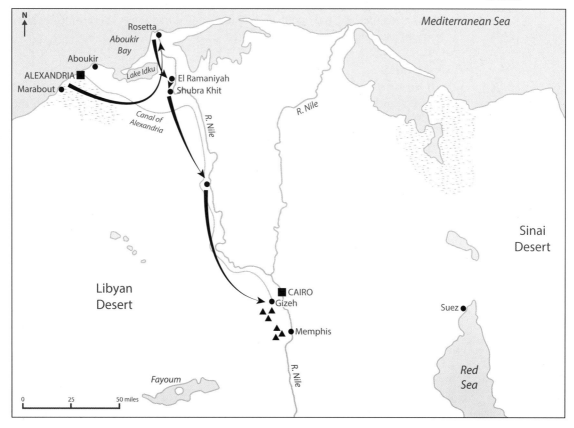

British mission to Constantinople, to summon Cairo. Belliard, having been strengthened by forces which *Général de Brigade* Donzelot had brought from Upper Egypt, by the various garrisons that had abandon their posts, and by Lagrange's force from Ramanieh, was in no mood to surrender. He marched for Belbeis with about 8,000 troops, confident of victory despite being heavily outnumbered. In the event the French failed to dislodge the Turks, who attacked them with their strongest arm, their cavalry, and Belliard was forced to withdraw in good order.

17 May

An Arab, arriving at 1:00 a.m., brought news to Hely-Hutchinson that a French detachment made up of a 200-strong dromedary corps, 330 infantry and sixty-nine gunners, was marching across the desert from Alexandria in an attempt to reach Cairo with supplies. Brigadier General Doyle volunteered to pursue them with his brigade and the cavalry. A hard march through sand, without provisions or water, brought the cavalry within sight of the French at 1:00 p.m. The infantry were still struggling through sand and failed to keep up. Doyle sent forward Major Wilson with a flag of truce. Having at first come under French fire, he was then able to persuade the convoy to surrender. The detachment had been escorting a train of over 400 camels. They had also been shadowed by a large body of Arabs who had harassed them over several days, which probably explains their readiness to surrender to the British. It is interesting to note that Doyle, in the account he sent to Hely-Hutchinson, bestowed particular praise on Wilson, whom he described as a zealous and active officer, but also on Colonel John Abercromby, whose activity and intelligence had ensured success.

19 May

News arrived of the Turkish success at El Khanka. Hely-Hutchinson sent the 30th and the 89th, along with cavalry and artillery detachments, to join the Turks.

21 May

Coote posted 200 hundred infantry from the Brigade of Guards, along with twenty cavalry and two guns, on the canal of Alexandria at Beda in order to maintain communications with the interior.

23 May

Hely-Hutchinson and the Captain Pacha set off to visit the Vizier, whose army was now at Benerhasset, in order to co-ordinate tactics. The troops suffered greatly from the effects of the khamsin, which was not only hot but also carried so much dust and sand that just breathing became a struggle.

24 May

The Vizier had ordered the construction of a pontoon bridge over the Nile to facilitate communication between the two armies and this now allowed Hely-Hutchinson and the Captain Pacha easy access to the Vizier's camp. They were received by the Vizier in his magnificent tent and treated with great distinction, which included allowing Hely-Hutchinson and his staff to sit in the Vizier's presence. The day culminated in a grand dinner, after which Hely-Hutchinson retired to a splendid tent of his own, guarded by janissaries.

25 May
Hely-Hutchinson had a meeting with the Vizier's council, during which plans were laid for the siege of Cairo. He was also given an array of valuable gifts by the Vizier.

29 May
The commander-in-chief returned to Algam.

30 May
A messenger from Osman Bey arrived with the news that the Mamelukes under his command were now on the march to unite with the British army. Hely-Hutchinson sent two of his aides-de-camp, Captains Taylor and Proby, to liaise with Osman Bey. The arrival of the Mamelukes made the French position more difficult. They had been depending on the cooperation of the local population but the influence of the Mamelukes would secure local support for the British.

1 June
At daylight the army continued their advance after a fortnight's respite at Algam, a decision that provoked more mutinous protests which Hely-Hutchinson ignored. A march of three miles brought the troops to Mishlee, where they were joined by over a thousand Mamelukes.

Coote received orders to send the 28th and 42nd Foot, 60 dragoons, and 120 gunners to join the main army in readiness for the siege.

4 June
The detachment set off under the command of Brigadier General Oakes, who was still not fully recovered from the wound he received on the 21 March. Their departure left Coote with only 5,000 men, over 1,500 of whom were suffering from ophthalmia or dysentery. There was also an outbreak of the plague in Aboukir.

6 June
Coote abandoned the post at Beda because he was so short of men.

A French ship, *l'Oiseau*, was taken as it sought to leave Alexandria for France, and brought into Aboukir Bay. Aboard were some of the *savants* whom Bonaparte had brought to Egypt. By this stage, they had had enough of the adventure and had asked for passage. Menou had willingly agreed, because these useless mouths, as he regarded them, were a drain on his limited resources. Keith understood this and ordered the ship to return to Alexandria.

7 June
The main army had left Mishlee on the 4 June and three days later was beyond El Gatta. The advance proceeded in three columns, with the Mamelukes on

the right, the British in the centre, and the Pacha's forces on the left. At the same time the Vizier's army advanced along the eastern branch of the Nile, taking pains to remain in parallel with Hely-Hutchinson.

Gantheaume, escorting five transports, had been hovering off the coast for some time, seemingly made cautious by the proximity of Keith's fleet. The plan was to land the men in the transports further along the coast, from where they could make their own way to Alexandria. When the five transports were seized, it was discovered that far from carrying soldiers, they were bringing actors, gardeners, and other such personnel, as if preparatory to the establishment of a French colony in Egypt. A corvette was more successful, managing to enter the harbour at Alexandria and land its cargo of ammunition.

8 June

An advance of three miles brought the allied army to Burtos, at the southernmost point of the Nile delta, while the Vizier's army reached Charlahan. This enabled easy communication between the two forces by means of another pontoon bridge across the Nile. It also meant the desert terrain changed into a fertile plain.

When Baird finally reached Kosseir, he learnt that the rest of his troops had been arriving there in detachments since the 17 May, including a force from the Cape of Good Hope.

10 June

The 86th Foot, 200 strong, joined Colonel Stewart's detachment, which was with the Vizier. This battalion was the first of Baird's troops to join the main army, having sailed from the Malabar Coast with Rear Admiral Blankett. Hely-Hutchinson had sent orders to Suez that they should join him. The Vizier had sent camels, and the march had taken three days.

13 June

Rear Admiral Sir Richard Bickerton, who had been searching for Gantheaume's dispersed squadron, returned to the main fleet without having located it, and it was assumed that the French admiral had returned to Toulon. This meant that Menou was unlikely to receive any more reinforcements.

14 June

Hely-Hutchison advanced his force three miles to a position that gave them their first clear view of the pyramids.

15 June

A message was sent to Belliard, commandant in Cairo, inviting him to surrender. He refused.

16 June

The main allied army now moved to a position where it was just out of reach of the guns in the defensive works that guarded Cairo. It was joined by the

A view of the Pyramids.
(Author's Collection)

28th and 42nd, along with the dragoons and gunners. The Vizier also moved forward, and again communications were maintained by a pontoon bridge.

The 13th Foot, which was sickly, replaced the 1/27th at Rosetta, the latter then marching for Cairo.

19 June

Baird's force commenced its march to Cairo (see Chapter 6)

20 June

The frigate HMS *Iphigenia* exploded in Aboukir Bay after a fire broke out at about 3:00 a.m. No lives were lost because her crew and passengers had been removed some time before.

21 June

Hely Hutchinson's force prepared to invest Gizeh, opposite Grand Cairo, while the Vizier as before took up a position close to the French outer defences on the other side of the Nile. Preparations were now made for the siege, and a depot was established close to the Nile so that the heavy guns and ammunition being brought up-river could be landed expeditiously. Cairo itself was virtually surrounded by allied troops. The forces of Hely-Hutchinson and the Pacha, as well as the Mamelukes, were on the western side, while the Vizier held ground to the west.

Major General Moore joined Coote's force from Rosetta, although, like Oakes, he was not fully recovered from the wound he received on the 21 March. He had also, according to Bunbury, managed to quash the plot against Hely-Hutchinson.

22 June

There was some reorganisation in the higher echelons of the British forces. Major General Cradock took overall command of the British troops in

A view of Gizeh. (Author's Collection)

the allied army and was replaced by Brigadier General Hope. Colonel Abercromby took over Hope's position as adjutant general, with Captain Taylor of the 25th as his deputy.

Belliard recognised that his situation was critical. He was nearly out of supplies and had no hope of reinforcements, while the morale of the men he did have was dangerously low. It is no wonder, therefore, that he shared the desolation of his own troops. Before the allied batteries could open up, he sent out a flag of truce, requesting that negotiations should begin for the French evacuation of Cairo. Hely-Hutchinson appointed Hope to meet with a French *général de brigade* the following day, after the Vizier had been consulted on the question of terms.

23 June

A first conference took place between Hope, Osman Bey (representing the Vizier) and Isaac Bey (representing the Captain Pacha) on the allied side and *Généraux de Brigade* Morand and Donzelot and *Chief of Brigade* Tareyre on the French. The emissaries made such good progress in their discussions that hostilities were quickly called off.

In the evening it was discovered that the French in Alexandria had let more water into the canal of Alexandria in order to flood the swampy ground between them and the British force, thus contracting their front.

24 June

Coote sent out vedettes to establish a position, after which 600 men were assembled in the evening to construct a dam, covered by 200 infantry, fifty cavalry and two light guns. The working party, which was joined by another

200 men at midnight, toiled all night, undisturbed by the French, who were engaged in making fresh cuts in the canal in order to increase the inundation. The British efforts proved the more successful.

26 June

Although his wound was still troubling him, Moore embarked in a germe for Cairo in the hope that he might become involved in what he assumed to be ongoing siege operations.

28 June

Terms had been agreed on the 27 June, and a convention was now signed for the surrender of Cairo within seventeen days. The garrison would then be transported down the Nile with their arms, baggage, and field artillery before being taken back to a French port in British ships. The allies agreed to meet the cost of this operation. After the convention had been signed, the allies took post at the gate of Gizeh and also occupied the Sulkowsky Fort on the Cairo side of the river.

Belliard subsequently justified his surrender in a fawning letter to Bonaparte in which he somewhat mendaciously acknowledged that the First Consul, who regarded the brave soldiers of Egypt as his children, had done what he could for them, but assistance had never arrived. For four months they had mounted a noble defence, contesting every inch of the ground, these warriors who bore the scars of Italy and Egypt, but eventually the plague, the weakness of their position, and the shortage of money and ammunition overwhelmed them. To say nothing of the enemy; but that is the point, he said nothing of the enemy.

29 June

Moore reached Cairo, only to discover that there had been no siege operations and the French had formally surrendered. When he subsequently inspected the defensive works, however, he came to the conclusion that a considerable amount of bloodshed had been avoided by the peaceful ending of this part of the campaign. He also realised that as soon as the French moved out, the Vizier would have to allow his troops into Cairo to plunder, since this was the reward they had been promised.

5 July

The frigate HMS *Leda* arrived in Aboukir Bay with 300 men of the 3rd Foot Guards and £15,000 pounds for the army. Pay had been seriously in arrears for some considerable time. It was also reported that further reinforcements had been about to leave England when the *Leda* set sail.

6 July

Menou received news that Cairo had surrendered. Although he was offered terms similar to those accepted by Belliard, he rejected them, claiming that death was preferable to surrender, a view that was probably not shared by most of his troops. He also refused to communicate with the British commanders by land, claiming that they had tried to encourage desertion.

As a result, communication was carried out by sea with flags of truce being sent from the British cruisers to the Pharos lighthouse.

8 July

The first of Baird's troops reached Kenneh, Baird himself arriving five days later. He halted, awaiting further orders from Hely-Hutchinson. When none were forthcoming, he began to think in terms of a withdrawal to the Red Sea.

9 July

The French withdrew from Cairo, which was immediately occupied by the 89th.

Major General Coote sailed off the coast of Alexandria in order to reconnoitre in preparation for the reduction of the city now that Cairo was in British hand. He took particular note of the narrowness of the neck of lane between the sea and the area that the French had flooded, which he decided could be held by no more than 5,000 men.

14 July

The 24th Foot, which had been expected by Coote for some time and the whereabouts of which were a cause for concern, arrived safely in Aboukir Bay.

15 July

The French left Cairo accompanied by a British force under the command of Moore, both Hely-Hutchinson and Cradock being indisposed. The 30th, which had been detached from Doyle's command to Stewart's on the 18 June, now re-joined the main army, while the 89th were left in garrison at Gizeh. The Vizier's army occupied Cairo. On the march the French followed the British, regulating their movements to the British. Their baggage was loaded on nearly 300 germes, one of which conveyed the body of the greatly respected Kléber, whose death was still lamented by the French.

16 July

Hely-Hutchinson received dispatches from Baird which informed him that the contingent from India had reached Kenneh, on the Nile.

18 July

A convoy from Minorca and Malta brought the two battalions of the 20th, the men having volunteered for Egypt despite being mainly for limited service. With them were the Ancient Irish Fencibles and the Löwenstein Jägers.

24 July

The arrival of the dismounted 22nd Light Dragoons brought Coote's force up to 9,000 effectives. Preparations were made for the French troops from Cairo, notification of their imminent arrival having been received some time before. In fact, despite the problems both generals encountered, communications between Hely-Hutchinson and Coote had been maintained throughout the advance on Cairo thanks to the good offices of some Bedouin Arabs.

Having changed his mind about withdrawing to the Red Sea, Baird began the march to Cairo, covering on average thirteen miles a day.

25 July
Both the French and the Anglo-Ottoman forces halted at Ramanieh, while at Rosetta Oakes supervised arrangements for the embarkation of the French.

28 July
The two forces reached El Hamed. By this point the French had lost much of their discipline in their eagerness to get back to France.

30 July
Hely-Hutchinson re-joined the army at Rosetta, although still far from recovered from his indisposition.

2 August
The embarkation of the French commenced on the 28 July when 600 hundred sick were brought up from Rosetta. Seven days later the last of the 4,500 troops, plus their guns and copious amounts of baggage were aboard ship.

3 August
Yet more reinforcements arrived in Aboukir Bay, 1,600 men of the Chasseurs Britanniques and de Watteville's from Malta and 120 gunners from Gibraltar.

7 August
Major General Coote was instructed by Hely-Hutchinson to send a flag of truce to the French outposts to make arrangements for the French paymaster-general, who had been in Cairo, to enter Alexandria and settle the army's accounts. Menou refused, sticking obstinately to his determination that there should be no communication by land.

Baird's force arrived at Gizeh, having completed the final stages of their journey by river.

9 August
The first of the Cairo forces, Doyle's brigade, reached Alexandria and was quickly followed by the rest of the Cairo troops. Hely-Hutchinson now united all his forces, totalling nearly 16,000 men, and decided upon the direction of the siege. He planned to invest the city from east and west. He also took the opportunity to reorganise the brigading of the army (see Appendix II).

11 August
The final division of the French troops from Cairo set sail from Aboukir Bay.

12 August
With the focus now on the reduction of Alexandria, general orders stated that a division of troops was to be posted to the west of the city under the

The defences of Alexandria.
(Author's Collection)

command of Major General Coote. The three brigades involved were the Guards under Cavan, the 1st under Ludlow and the 2nd under Finch.

13 August

Twenty-four gunboats were anchored in line across the area flooded by the French, whose gunboats were made useless by this manoeuvre. Moore brought the Reserve into camp and the arrival of this force, combined with the position of the gunboats, convinced Menou that he was about to be attacked. In response, he kept his troops under arms all night.

15 August

Hely-Hutchinson, who had been aboard HMS *Foudroyant* since the 2 August, came ashore to take overall command of the prosecution of the siege.

16 August

At 7:00 p.m. Coote's three brigades began to embark in naval boats and some Turkish gunboats in order to cross the inundation. They set sail at 9:30 p.m. but were dispersed when the wind changed direction.

17 August

At 10:00 a.m., after the boats had been collected together, the flotilla made for the shore. Coote then became aware that about 300 of the enemy, with two pieces of flying artillery, were posted on hills above the intended landing place. He ordered Major General Finch to make a diversion at the chosen landing place, thus keeping the French occupied while the other two brigades disembarked safely two miles further west and established a strong position along a ridge of steep quarries. In response, the French set fire to two of their gunboats, intending that they should drift into the line of British gunboats, but they blew up before they made contact with the British vessels. They also posted vedettes close to the British position, with yet more of their cavalry on the plain behind.

Hely-Hutchinson had ordered an attack on the French lines to the east of Alexandria, to commence at 4:00 a.m. It would serve as a diversion from Coote's activities but would also push the British line further forward. The main point of attack was a sand hill, facetiously called the green hill, a little to the front right of the French position. This was to be carried by Doyle's brigade, with the 30th marching up to a small redoubt on the right, the 50th to another on the left, and the 92nd to remain in the centre in order to give support where needed. The 1/20th and 2/20th were in position to offer further support if necessary. Although the green hill was carried without opposition, a position occupied by the Reserve under Moore, called the Sugarloaf Hill, was then abandoned as impossible to hold without heavy losses. This encouraged the French to attack the troops at the green hill. The 75e Demi-Brigade advanced with bayonets fixed on the 30th. The battalion, under 200 strong, and confronted by a force reckoned to be about 600, did not wait for the French to reach them. Led by Colonel Lockhart, they charged the enemy and drove them back to their entrenchments. It seems to have been a salutary lesson for the French because, although they kept up a cannonade, there were no further attacks.

18 August

By morning a battery of guns was in position to the right front of the British position to the east of Alexandria, while the redoubt to the right of the green hill was defended against French enfilading fire. At 2:00 a.m. there had been an attack on the outposts to the left and right of the British lines, but it was prosecuted with insufficient force to be effective.

To the west of the city, Coote advanced his brigades two miles further forward, meeting only the lightest opposition. He took up a position by which the Guards were in two lines with their right against the inundation, and Ludlow's and Finch's Brigades were formed *en potence*, against the sea.

19 August

At daybreak Coote opened a battery of two 12-pounders and two 8-inch howitzers against Fort Marabout, located on an island off Alexandria. This cannonade sank two French gunboats and drove a third into harbour.

20 August

While Coote waited for the construction of a battery of two 24-pounders, he posted the 1/54th to cover the siege of the fort. Colonel Darby, in command, pushed his light company so far forward on a spit of land that the French were unable even to raise their heads above the parapet, which meant they could not fire on the British positions.

Hely-Hutchinson was joined by the Turkish force under the command of the Captain Pacha. About 200 were posted to join the British troops on the green hill and the remainder were with the advanced position of the British right.

21 August

To the west the heavy guns, having been dragged over extremely rough ground by four battalions, were in position by daybreak and quickly opened fire on Fort Marabout. At 11:00 a.m. the fort's signal tower was brought down. Despite this, the French re-hoisted the flag and continued to return fire, but only randomly because of the accuracy of the British guns. Coote decided that since the French seemed disinclined to surrender, he would storm the fort during the night. This carried considerable risk so during the evening he sent his aide-de-camp, Thomas Walsh, and Colonel Darby to summon the commandant. There had been a change of heart inside the fort and the French were now willing to discuss terms for a capitulation. The discussions soon brought about a formal surrender.

22 August

Hely-Hutchinson had dispatched the 6th Brigade to join Coote but upon receiving information that Menou had decided to attack the troops to the west of Alexandria before the brigade could arrive he decided upon a diversionary attack from the east.

23 August

At 4:00 a.m. the French picquets were driven in, the British advanced in column, and the Turks took the Sugarloaf Hill. Five or six men were lost to the French guns, which opened fire before retiring.

At much the same time the 6th Brigade, under the temporary command of Colonel Spencer, landed to the west, while 250 Mamelukes came in from the desert. Later in the day 700 Turks from the Captain Pacha's force, took position behind the 6th Brigade. Hely-Hutchinson, accompanied by Cradock and the chief engineer, also came across to inspect Coote's position. He decided the siege would most propitiously be directed from the west. To further protect Coote's position, ten or twelve British ships formed line in the harbour. The French answered this move by sinking several of their oldest ships as a barrier against a landing from the sea.

24 August

Menou wrote to Hely-Hutchinson, thanking him for the care given to his wife, resident in Cairo and whom the Turks wished to decapitate as a renegade for taking a French husband. She had subsequently been sent into Alexandria. It was originally thought that the letter was a tentative move towards peace, particularly as it had been delivered by land, but there was no follow up.

25 August

Coote opened fire from two batteries on the Redoubt des Bains, whereupon the French returned fire from the redoubt, although without doing any damage beyond one man wounded. Coote was now anxious to get his guns closer to the redoubt in order to cause more damage. After darkness had fallen, he sent the 1/20th and a detachment of the 26th Light Dragoons, supported from the sand hills by the 2/54th, to drive in the French outposts. The attack was conducted with the bayonet and resulted in 100 French casualties, killed, wounded or taken prisoner. The British suffered just one officer and three men wounded. The French then attempted to counter-attack but finally withdrew at midnight without being able to dislodge their opponents.

26 August

Four batteries opened up on the French entrenchments from the east and quickly silenced some French counter-fire. At 4:30 p.m. one of Menou's aides-de-camp arrived at an advance post on the west with a letter for Major General Coote. Its contents proved to be a request for a cessation of hostilities for twenty-four hours. Coote sent the letter to Hely-Hutchinson and ceased all activity, as did the French, until the commander-in-chief's reply should be received.

27 August

Hely-Hutchinson's reply, received at 1:00 a.m., agreed to the French request and white flags were flown to signal this to Menou.

29 August

It had been expected that Menou would now accept terms for a capitulation, but when an aide-de-camp arrived late in the afternoon, the message he brought requested an extension of the truce. This request was refused and Coote prepared to renew hostilities at midnight. Menou, however, realising that he would not get what he wanted, moderated his demand and asked for truce until 2:00 p.m. the following afternoon.

30 August

At 2:00 p.m. an aide-de-camp brought in Menou's proposals for the capitulation but the conditions he was making were considered unacceptable. For example, he expected to retain French shipping in the harbour and all public property, as well as making a condition that if a relief force should arrive by the 17 September he was at liberty to continue the fight. Hely-Hutchinson responded that he must moderate his demands or hostilities would be resumed. Menou then sent another aide-de-camp who offered a more accommodating arrangement and the truce continued.

31 August

Baird had remained at Gizeh until the 28 August, when he received orders to bring his force to Rosetta. Because the Nile was in full flood, his army reached Rosetta in three days, but as at Cairo it was too late to see any action.

2 September

Menou finally accepted and signed terms similar to those he had been offered nearly two months before. At midday the British formally took possession of the French lines, which had been evacuated shortly before.

As Thomas Walsh, reflecting on the moment, wrote in 1803:

The day was extremely fine and the whole scene, heightened by the reflections, which must have arisen in very breast on the termination of a glorious campaign, was certainly one of the most pleasing and gratifying that a soldier can feel… An enemy who during the war had considered himself as invincible, was taught by this campaign, that British troops, meeting him on fair ground, will ever maintain a fair superiority. From it we hope will result some advantage to our country; and we trust that it will not be easily forgotten, either by our enemies, or by our friends.[2]

For Menou it was necessary to blame someone. When advocating surrender to his council of war, he claimed that the loss of Cairo had led directly to their present situation, with the inevitable consequence that Alexandria would be taken if they did not now capitulate. Cairo should have held out for at least another two months, he claimed, during which period provisions might have been got into Alexandria and the extra fortifications that he had ordered might have been completed. Excuses made no difference, though. By 20 October, the last Frenchman had departed from Egypt. The campaign had achieved its objective.

---

2   Thomas Walsh, *Journal of the Campaign in Egypt* (London: T.Cadwell & W. Davies, 1803), pp.234-235.

6

The British Army in Action

The Aboukir Landings, 8 March 1801

In preparation for the landings, on the 3 March the bomb ships, HMS *Tartarus* and HMS *Fury*, were anchored close in to Aboukir Bay, but out of range of French guns.

Unfortunately, contrary conditions meant this first move could not be followed up for some time; time during which it became apparent to the British that the French were erecting batteries on the sand hills.

The troops chosen for the first line were the Reserve and the Guards, along with the 2/1st (Royals) and both battalions of the 54th from the 1st Brigade. They would be supported by 10 pieces of cannon, manned by the appropriate number of gunners. On the 6 March, with the landings projected for the following day, Abercromby issued a general order by which the

'View of the Castle of Aboukir with the disposition of the Boats previous to the landing'. (Anne S.K. Brown Military Collection)

soldiers in the first line were to take with them their blankets, three days provisions, and entrenching tools, while their knapsacks were to be left aboard ship. The weather again played tricks, and the landings were delayed for another twenty-four hours, but this allowed Abercromby to add a further refinement to the arrangements. On the evening of the 7 March, he issued another general order by which the troops of the second line transferred to the ships with the lowest draught, which could come closer inshore. Thus the second wave of landings would follow more rapidly on the first.

At 2:00 a.m. on the 8 March, a rocket signal was fired and the boats moved towards their appointed ships. An hour later, a further signal instructed the launches and gunboats covering the landings to assemble by *Tartarus*. And by 3:30 a.m. the troops were in the boats, 50 men per flat boat with sailors to row, while the naval boats were either towing the flat boats or carrying troops. In total five thousand soldiers sat in the bottom of the boats with their muskets between their knees. The boats moved towards the rendezvous, indicated by three armed vessels stationed in line opposite the shore and out of French gunshot reach. Naval captains now directed the boats so that they observed the appropriate distances, according to the order of battle. This placed the Reserve on the right, with the other boats dressing by them.

Major General Moore, in command of the reserve, received an order from Abercromby, carried to him by the adjutant general, John Hope. This warned him that if the commander-in-chief judged that the enemy fire was too severe, he would give a signal to retire. Moore and Alexander Cochrane, directing naval operations, were to watch for this. Abercromby also expressed some continuing concern about the steepness of the central sand hill, but Moore sent a message back with the confident assurance that the hill could be ascended and no change of plan was necessary. It was noticed that several times during the landings that Abercromby slightly raised his hand, as if to give the signal for withdrawal, but then let it fall to his side. He had never been a general who could turn a blind eye to the waste of men's lives.

The sailors lowered the oars, and the boats moved forward, supported by light vessels armed with carronades. For the men watching, this was an awe-inspiring moment of solemn silence, the only sound the gentle splash of oars dipping into water as the boats steadily rowed about five miles towards the shore to take up their final positions. Soon after 8:00 a.m. they were in line and Captain Cochrane gave the order to advance towards the shore, maintaining the line for as long as was possible, just as had been practised at Marmaris Bay. Immediately there was a sense of eagerness in soldiers and sailors alike.

It was probably at this point that many of the men contemplated for the first time the point of disembarkation which an officer of the 40th described as narrow, and dominated by a sand hill that commanded the whole landing area, although the beach actually extended for about a mile, with a sixty degree curve in the centre. This sand hill was considered inaccessible because of its steepness, and the unstable nature of the sand itself. On either side were smaller sand hills which extended to the limits of the French position in the form of Aboukir Castle on the right, fronted by thick scrub, and a blockhouse on the left. Between these smaller hills the French commander in Alexandria, *Général de Division* Louis Friant, had posted more troops and guns. To many, the beach must have looked impregnable.

As the advance passed them, the two bomb ships, *Tartarus* and *Fury*, began to throw shells ashore, fire which was supported by two gunboats and three armed launches, while from behind the waiting men of the second line the naval ships brought their guns into play. For a moment there was no response. Then the French, who could now be seen standing by their guns, replied with a sudden outburst of well-managed fire from fifteen cannon on the sand hills, and more from Aboukir Castle. Firstly they chose shot but as the boats drew ever closer they changed to grape and langrage, which fell upon the boats like a violent hail storm on water. Every man was vulnerable, lacking the means to defend himself. Three boats were sunk, including one carrying some of the Coldstreamers, which was destroyed by a shell. Yet the British response was a chorus of cheering and huzzaing, while the cutters of the fleet saved as many of the floundering men as possible.

Just before 9:00 a.m. the first boats touched bottom, rather sooner than had been anticipated because of the shallowness of the bay. This was a moment of anxious doubt. Everything depended upon how the troops behaved in the next few minutes. The men scrambled out and immediately formed up, despite being subjected to small arms fire from those French who had ventured down from the sand hills, and which did much mischief. Indeed, some of the British soldiers were already loading their muskets as they left the boats and immediately returned fire. An eyewitness described the first landings as a fluid advance from boats to shore, and then to the summit of

The landings at Aboukir.
(Author's Collection)

the dominant sand hill. The first into action, led by Moore, were the 23rd, the 28th and the flank companies of the 40th. Having quickly formed up and repulsed the French with the bayonet, they charged towards the highest sand hill and began the difficult ascent. Some few marched. Most crawled on hands and knees. Although under fire from the French, they made no attempt to return fire as they climbed, a sign of men in control of themselves. Finally, they reached the summit, where the French 61e Demi-Brigade was in position to receive them. Unnerved by the intrepidity of the charge, these troops panicked and retreated, abandoning their two six-pounders. The Reserve followed them until they reached favourable ground, where they halted and looked to see what was happening elsewhere.

By now a force of French cavalry, their presence hitherto unsuspected, had debouched from behind the sand hills and Oakes, landing with the 43rd, 58th, and the Corsican Rangers, found both infantry and cavalry waiting for him. He was quickly able to form up his battalions and see off the threat; but the cavalry now switched attention to his left and charged the Guards and 2/1st of Ludlow's and Coote's brigades as they scrambled ashore. With Oakes in support, these troops were able to steady themselves and hold off the cavalry, who then decided, as more and more British troops landed, that retreat was the better part of valour.

Aboukir Bay and the eastern approaches to Alexandra.

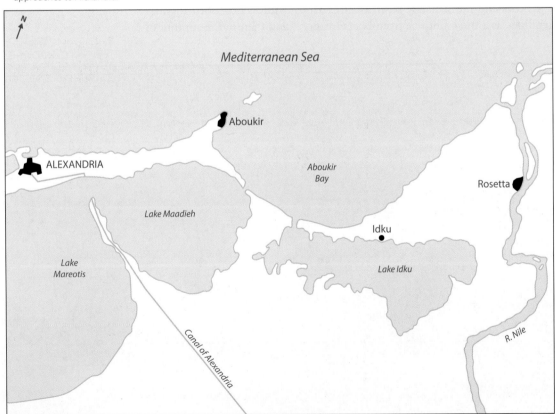

Within twenty minutes the defenders were giving way at all points, leaving the British to take possession of the dunes. Also, by this time, some sailors, who were being directed by Sir Sidney Smith, were dragging up some of the British guns. This was enough to send the French into full retreat along Lake Maadieh (Lake Aboukir) on to Mandorah, which was about four miles from the beach. The 51e Demi-Brigade, however, was sent to strengthen the garrison of the castle.

The result of the French withdrawal was that the British second line landed unopposed and the whole force was able to occupy that ground vacated by the French. A foothold had been secured as the first stage of the campaign. As Moore pertinently wrote in his journal, the French had had eight days to assemble their troops and secure the ground in a position that was highly favourable to defence. In response, the British troops had executed a daring move with intrepidity and coolness.

The defending force comprised about 2,500 men in total. They lost 400 men killed, wounded or prisoners, and six guns and a howitzer. General Martinet was among those killed.

British losses were 643 soldiers and 97 sailors killed, wounded or missing.

Army casualties:
Killed: 4 officers, 4 sergeants, 94 rank and file
Wounded: 26 officers, 34 sergeants, 5 drummers, 450 rank and file
Missing: 1 officer, 1 sergeant, 1 drummer, 23 rank and file

Naval casualties:
Killed: 22 sailors
Wounded: 7 officers, 65 sailors
Missing: 33 sailors

On the 9 March Abercromby opened his general order with unstinting praise:

The gallant behaviour of the troops in the action yesterday claims, from the Commander-in-Chief, the warmest praise that he can bestow; and it is with particular satisfaction that he observed their conduct, marked equally for ardent bravery and by coolness, regularity, and order.[1]

They had behaved exactly as he believed a well-trained and well-motivated army should.

Mandorah, 13 March 1801

Aboukir had given the army confidence. One young soldier in the 92nd, experiencing his first campaign, believed the landings would quickly be followed up, with yet more success, because they were under the command

---

1   Walsh, *Journal*, Appendix No.4, p.14.

and had the guidance of the gallant Sir Ralph Abercromby. This spirit and self-belief, which Abercromby had instilled, would carry his force close to the walls of Alexandria.

The day after the successful landings, Abercromby sent Major General John Moore and the Quartermaster General, Colonel Robert Anstruther, to find an advanced position for the army. Having probed the French lines, the two men decided on a narrow neck of ground between the sea and Lake Maadieh, marked by a small redoubt and a flagpole, which the French had abandoned. This won Abercromby's approval, and Moore was instructed to hold it with the Reserve, while the main body formed up in three lines, the Guards, Coote's and Finch's brigades comprising the first, Cradock's and Cavan's, the second, and Stuart's and Doyle's, the third.

Initially, the French opposed Moore's forward movement with their cavalry, but were seen off by the Corsican Rangers. Unfortunately, the Corsicans then advanced too far and were attacked by some of the main body of the French, which had been screened by the cavalry. This cost the Corsicans Lieutenant Guittera, Surgeon Smith, and 13 rank and file, all taken prisoner. The French continued to fire on the Reserve, but when Moore ordered his own troops to cease fire, the bickering died away and the French retired.

On 11 March Abercromby inspected the position but also realised that the army could not advance to join the Reserve until sufficient supplies had been landed. This had been impossible for the past two days because of the capricious weather conditions. On that very day, however, supplies for three

The action at Mandorah, 13 March 1801: first phase.

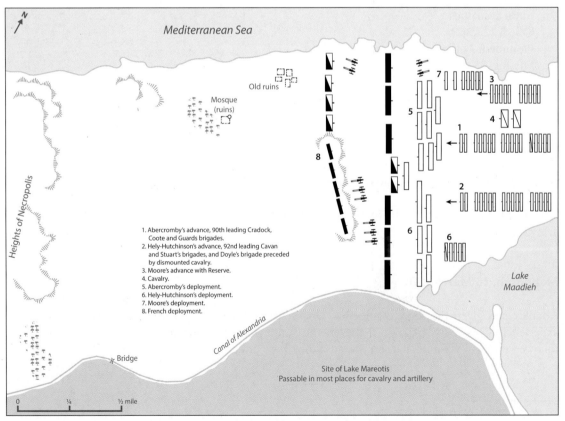

1. Abercromby's advance, 90th leading Cradock, Coote and Guards brigades.
2. Hely-Hutchinson's advance, 92nd leading Cavan and Stuart's brigades, and Doyle's brigade preceded by dismounted cavalry.
3. Moore's advance with Reserve.
4. Cavalry.
5. Abercromby's deployment.
6. Hely-Hutchinson's deployment.
7. Moore's deployment.
8. French deployment.

Mediterranean Sea

Old ruins

Mosque (ruins)

Heights of Necropolis

Bridge

Canal of Alexandria

Lake Maadieh

Site of Lake Mareotis
Passable in most places for cavalry and artillery

0   ¼   ½ mile

days were finally brought ashore, and the army received the order to march the following morning at 8:00 a.m., having first filled their canteens with water, which was fresh even within a short distance of the sea. Each line formed two columns, and in this formation they advanced across a landscape of sand and palm trees, led by the Guards on the right and Coote's brigade on the left, screened by 50 dragoons from Finch's brigade. When they caught up with the Reserve, which had been waiting for them in their position of the previous evening, the whole force marched further forward, headed by Moore and Oakes' battalions. At one point they came across a post that the French had hastily abandoned, leaving signal flags and colours flying. These were immediately replaced by British flags.

More distressing for inexperienced soldiers was the sight of bleached bodies, victims of one of Bonaparte's battles.

The ground had now changed to deeper sand and scrub, which made progress more difficult. Good order was preserved, though, and this persuaded some French infantry, who had been moving forward, to retire. A mile further on, and the British had a clear view of the French drawn up along a ridge of sand hills. Their lines extended from Lake Maadieh to the sea, where it was anchored by some old ruins. It was now early afternoon, and Abercromby chose to call a halt for the day. The British took up a position which meant the French outposts were immediately in their front, while the main bodies of the two armies were about three miles apart. There was some sporadic gunfire on both sides, and also some skirmishing between the British advanced posts and French vedettes which lasted until dusk. Moore, the subordinate Abercromby relied upon before all others, was ordered to take command of the advanced posts and cover the army with the two junior battalions, the 90th and the 92nd, from Cradock's and Coote's brigades. Moore formed then into a strong chain, so that a third of each battalion spent an hour at the front, acting as sentries, before being relieved by another third. This was a difficult night for inexperienced soldiers. They were not allowed to remove their knapsacks, or to lie down and make themselves too comfortable.

Both sides had now received reinforcements. At sunset all but the flank companies of the 2nd (Queen's) had set off from Aboukir Castle, accompanied by 500 marines. They had reached the main army by midnight, having directed themselves by distant lights, which proved to be the fires that extended along their whole line. On the French side, two and a half brigades of infantry and a cavalry regiment had arrived from Cairo, in advance of a force Menou was bringing to the relief of Alexandria.

The army remained at arms all night because Abercromby had already decided to attack the enemy the following morning, his plan being to turn the French right. On 13 March, a Friday for those who were superstitious, the men received a ration of rum and were ordered to remove knapsacks, which were guarded by the weakest soldiers. The intention had been to move forward at 5:00 a.m. but it was not until 6:30 a.m. that the British advanced in two columns by the left. Cavan's brigade was led by the 92nd and to their right, and slightly ahead, Cradock's brigade was led by the 90th. Coote was following up in support of Cradock, the Reserve was in two columns near the sea, supported by the Guards; Stuart's and Doyle's brigades, along with the dismounted cavalry, followed Cavan.

The two leading battalions were acting as 'riflemen' according to one soldier, by which he meant they were in skirmish order. Marching in extended line, they were soon in danger of losing touch with the main force. Consequently, they were the first to suffer when the French initiated a combined arms attack, firstly against the 90th, who, having no time to get into line, responded with the coolness of veterans and repulsed them with the bayonet. Then, as the French wheeled about, they received a volley which rattled like a peal of thunder and sent them into precipitous retreat.

The 92nd were next attacked, by the 61e Demi-Brigade and two field pieces firing grape. They continued their advance undeterred. Then, realising that the French intended to cut them off, they deployed five companies into line, while the other five were held among the scrub to the left. Private Nicol in his journal described the French advance as like the blade of a scythe, the point of the blade comprised of cavalry, which was to swing round and take them in the rear while the rest of the force launched a frontal attack. Their commanding officer, Colonel Erskine, who would suffer a mortal wound later in the action, ordered them to stand firm and not fire until they could see the feet of the enemy. Then they hit the French with a steady, precise volley, although Nicol admits that most of the men were firing and praying at the same time. The first volley brought the French advance to a halt and then there was a static fire fight which produced so much smoke that the enemy was soon hidden from view.

They were finally relieved when the supporting columns came up, although they were also taking casualties from the French flying artillery, which was able to enfilade deep into their ranks. In response, they deployed into line with the utmost speed and precision, leaving only the Reserve and Doyle's brigade still in column. Not before the 90th had taken about 400 casualties, and the 92nd, about 200, however. They now lay down so that the 2/27th and 79th could pass over them and take up the fight.[2] Then they moved to the left where Dillon's Regiment was engaged by the Mandorah tower. From this position Dillon's successfully attacked a French cavalry force and took the two supporting guns that were trained against them.

Up to this point, armed naval boats on Lake Maadieh had been keeping pace with the advance on the left of the army, but the water was now too shallow and their support was lost.

The action soon became general, although any advance by the British inevitably had to slow down while the sailors, with Sir Sidney Smith in command, hauled the guns into position. The French took advantage of the delay to bring up their guns and inflict yet more casualties, only to retire as soon as the British were once more on the move. When the second line turned the French right and drove them out of position, the whole French force was pushed back under the cover of their guns, which still halted at

---

2   This is from David Robertson, *Journal of Sergeant D. Robertson, Late 92nd Foot* (Perth: J. Fisher, 1842), p.19, who refers to the 17th and 79th. Since the 17th were not even in Egypt, it must be inferred that this is a typographical error in the original and that the 27th was meant.

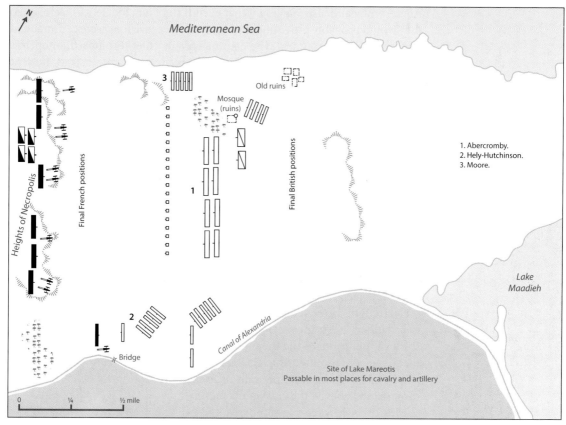

Mediterranean Sea

Old ruins

Mosque
(ruins)

3

Final French positions

Final British positions

Heights of Necropolis

1. Abercromby.
2. Hely-Hutchinson.
3. Moore.

1

Lake
Maadieh

2

Canal of Alexandria

Bridge

Site of Lake Mareotis
Passable in most places for cavalry and artillery

0   ¼   ½ mile

The action at Mandorah,
13 March 1801: second phase.

intervals to fire on the pursuers. Moore held the Reserve in column to cover the British right flank, and later reported that they had remained in perfect order, despite losses to the French guns, and could have instantly wheeled to a flank, should it have proved necessary. By now the British were ascending rising ground and could see the French retreating in some confusion, although they had hitherto retired in good order. Their objective was the heavily fortified Heights of Necropolis, under the walls of Alexandria, a position anchored by two forts, Cafarelli and Cretin.

Moore halted the Reserve, Cradock did the same with his brigade, and they waited for the rest of the army to come up. A further forward movement would have been foolhardy until they knew Abercromby's intentions.

Initially, Abercromby ordered a general advance, but it was then discerned that the French had retired to a strong position and were now forming up defensively. There followed a consultation between the commander, his official second-in-command, Hely-Hutchinson, and the man who might be described as his preferred second-in-command, even if he was too junior for the position, John Moore. As a result of their discussion, Hely-Hutchinson was sent with some of the second line to attack the French right, while the Reserve and the Brigade of Guards attacked the French left close to the sea. Hely-Hutchinson had further to march, so the attack was delayed until he was in position. He made an initial attack but quickly realised that he would be able to take ground only with considerable losses. He reported this to

Abercromby and also suggested that even if the French defences were taken they would probably prove impossible to hold because they were commanded by the guns in Alexandria. The commander-in-chief recognised a hopeless situation and immediately abandoned the planned attack. Instead, he sent Hope to inspect the position, and examined it himself with a telescope. It has been suggested with some validity that his short-sightedness had initially caused him to misjudge the situation, although the heat haze seems to have misled Hutchinson and Moore as well and only Hely-Hutchinson's reconnaissance to the sand hill had revealed the true situation.

All this while the army had been under accurate French gunfire, both shot and grape, and was taking unnecessary casualties. It was obvious the French had recovered their élan. Furthermore, the day was wearing on. Abercromby gave the order to withdraw to the original French position. Yet once again the British force had showed spirit and determination; the men would have been ready to continue the fight if so ordered. Unfortunately, this did not compensate for the French superiority in cavalry and, even more significantly, artillery. Furthermore, the British guns constantly lagged behind as naval personnel dragged them through deep sand to the best of their strength. However, men were not horses, and the artillery horses had yet to be landed. Nevertheless, Moore could write in his journal, 'the undaunted spirit of the troops made them constantly advance in spite of every loss, so that we gained ground, which is the great object of every action'.[3] The French had been driven back to the walls of Alexandria, and those of an optimistic disposition believed the city would soon fall.

The British force outnumbered the French nearly two to one (about 13,000 to 7,000), but this was more than compensated from the French perspective by their superiority in cavalry and artillery. In any engagement, the British would have to confront 600 well-mounted cavalry with 250 poorly mounted light dragoons, while the French had 40, mainly curricle, highly manoeuvrable, guns against a much smaller number of British guns which were dependent on manpower to move them.

Army losses:
Killed: 6 officers; 6 sergeants; 1 drummer; 143 rank and file; 21 horses
Wounded: 66 officers (5 later returned 'since dead'); 1 quartermaster; 61 sergeants; 7 drummers; 946 rank and file; 5 horses
Missing: 1 rank and file

Naval losses (under the command of Sir Sidney Smith):
Killed: 5 sailors
Wounded: 1 midshipman; 19 sailors

Marine losses:
Killed: 2 officers; 22 rank and file
Wounded: 4 officers; 2 sergeants; 2 drummers; 27 rank and file

---

3   Sir John Moore, (ed. J.F. Maurice), *The Diary of Sir John Moore* (London: Edward Arnold, 1904). Vol.II, p.9.

The French losses seem have been lighter; one staff officer reckoned they would have amounted to no more than 700.

The Battle of Alexandria, 21 March 1801

After the successful advance on the French position outside Alexandria, which culminated in the action at Mandorah, Abercromby established his force in the two lines that would be maintained until the next encounter with the French. The first line comprised the Reserve, a little advanced on the right and by the sea, the Guards and Coote's brigade in the centre, and Cradock on the left. They were on flat ground extending to the canal of Alexandria, which separated Lake Maadieh from Lake Mareotis. The latter was dry at this time of year, although how firm had not yet been established. In the second line, Stuart's brigade was on the right, Doyle's in the centre, and Cavan's on the left. In reserve was the cavalry, posted in a hollow where the Aboukir to Alexandria road passed between the Guards and the Reserve. The weakest point was the left because of the plain to front and rear.

Abercromby now concentrated on strengthening this position by throwing up a line of works and fortifying the structures that already existed. At each end of the line was a redoubt, not quite complete because each was still open at the rear. The one on the right lay in front of the ruins which the French called Caesar's Camp (although a knowledgeable British officer thought it was more likely the palace or library of Ptolemy) and was armed with two 24-pounders. The one on the left guarded the canal with two 12-pounders. In addition, several fleches armed with one or two guns punctuated the line, the one in the centre, on raised ground, being described by a soldier of the 92nd as a grand battery. From this height it was possible to inspect all the fortifications of Alexandria. The men were also set to work bringing up baskets of earth to raise the breast works, while entrenchments were formed against cavalry. Once the heavy guns and ammunition started to come ashore, a depot was established to accommodate them. This engendered the confident expectation among the troops that Alexandria was the next objective and would soon be taken, while John Moore, not given to pie in the sky expectations, conceded that the guns brought immeasurable strength to their position and made them tolerably secure.

Thanks to the efforts of the sailors, tents were finally being landed and offered protection both from the sun at its height and the evening dews. Another comfort for officers and men alike was the arrival of the local Arabs with fresh food, fruit and vegetables, meat on the hoof (including ostriches, according to one soldier), and horses. One officer believed that the Arabs were offering this help to the British in response to the unrelenting barbarity of the French. George Baldwin, long-time consul in Egypt, had been with the army since Marmaris to provide local information. He now took command of the market that was quickly established and ran it with ardent zeal, setting prices and opening hours. In a general order Abercromby directed that officers and men alike could only purchase articles at the set prices and at the times specified. There was to be no bargaining on the side, and there

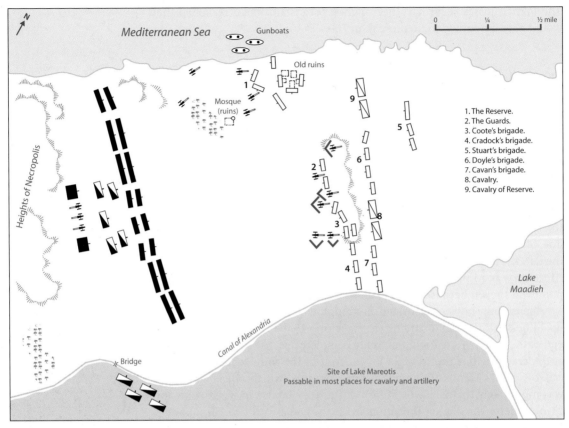

The Battle of Alexandria, 21 March 1801.

would be harsh punishment for any transgressors, particularly if there were suspicions of coercion or theft. This was a reminder to the army that Abercromby expected them to treat the local inhabitants with respect. It was in line with his determination that discipline and readiness for action must be maintained at all times, these being what he regarded as the two most vital characteristics of a successful army.

This amity between the British and the local inhabitants did not please the French and on 18 March a reconnaissance party was sent out to the canal of Alexandria before daybreak to stop the Arabs from coming to the British lines. They were quick to use violence to effect their purpose. In response, the 12th and 26th Light Dragoons, under Lieutenant Colonel Archdall, saddled up and attacked the French, taking several prisoners. They pursued them too far, however, and came under fire from some French infantry, concealed behind the parapet of an old redoubt. Despite the intervention of the Minorca Regiment, which had hurried up in support, the British lost 33 men and 42 horses, killed, wounded or taken prisoner, and Archdall lost an arm. In a subsequent general order Abercromby made clear that officers commanding detached parties, having obtained their objective, were to resist the temptation to act precipitously in pursuit of foolish or purposeless enterprises. He also ordered that from now on the troops were to be under arms an hour before daybreak and not dismissed until an hour after. The men were also ordered to keep their arms and accoutrements by them at all times.

During this period of stasis there was some bickering between British and French vedettes, and one tragedy when Colonel Brice of the Coldstreamers lost his way in the dark while doing the rounds and was shot. The French carried him off and tended his wounds but he died soon after. Having some occasion to write to Général de Division Friant, Abercromby suggested that both sides should desist from acts that gave no benefit to the general cause but caused individuals to suffer. In reply, Friant concurred with Abercromby's sentiments.

The Castle of Aboukir had been under blockade since the successful landings. The commandant had refused the repeated offers of an honourable surrender sent in by the British commander of the blockade, Colonel Lord Dalhousie. On the 17th, the walls having been breached, he finally accepted the British terms, which allowed the French to keep their personal possessions. They marched out with the honours of war and boarded British ships for the voyage back to France. The end of the blockade released the flank companies of the 2nd (Queen's) to join the main army. It also meant there was no longer a French position that could potentially menace the British rear. At the same time, Abercromby looked at his force and decided that the 92nd, weakened by their losses at Mandorah, affected by the first indications of opthalmia, and mustering only 250 men fit for duty, should be sent to Aboukir where they could receive the better provisions which would help them to recuperate. The decision was not put into immediate effect, however.

Despite all these positive developments, Abercromby's position was a challenging one. He was 1,000 leagues from home. If the army were defeated, it would be totally lost. He was opposed by Bonaparte's undefeated Army of Italy which bore names like Lodi, Arcola, and Rivoli on their standards, an army blessed with numerous and admirably appointed artillery, and cavalry of the finest description mounted on Arabian horses. For Moore the challenge seemed insuperable, because even if the French were ejected form their present position – and that was challenge enough – Alexandria would still have to be taken. He concluded it was mortifying that so much good spirit and so many valuable lives would have to be expended without obtaining their objective. He suspected that Abercromby shared his doubts, knowing as he did that gallantry alone could not overwhelm strongly defended fortifications. What was more, when Menou arrived the British would be outnumbered.

In fact, Abercromby had devised a possible next move. If the artillery were to be pushed forward during the night, and the troops were formed under whatever cover could be found, it would be possible to launch a daylight attack on both French flanks. If that failed, though, they would have to withdraw to their present position, and defend it until another had been prepared in the rear to make retreat and re-embarkation possible. Yet he confessed himself loth to throw away such a fine army on what would then be yet another pointless campaign.

Friant had 7,000 men at most, even though they had been reinforced by Lanusse's division. The unresolved issue at this point was the whereabouts of Menou. It was possible that he was already at Damanhur, within reach of Alexandria, with the other half of the Army of Egypt. Finally, on 20 March, troops of camels and other animals were observed in the vicinity of Alexandria. Menou himself arrived at noon with 9,000 men. On the same day Abercromby issued a general order instructing the troops 'to be in readiness to turn out at a moment's warning' should the enemy launch a night attack. He continued:

> The troops must be fully conscious of the glory which they have already acquired, and their superiority over the enemy whom they have so often beat; but at the same time, prudence and discipline must be strongly recommended and enforced. With a little caution, the British army in Egypt will find that they are invincible.[4]

Nevertheless, there was no expectation among the British that the French would launch a full attack against what was now a strongly entrenched position. In this they were wrong. The French commander was determined to drive the British back to their ships. He had a plan which he was sure could not fail, and he expected to take the enemy by surprise. For the first time, the French would be on the offensive on their own terms rather than reacting to a British advance, a change that suited them temperamentally and tactically.

After the battle, Menou's general orders issued on the 20 March were found in General Roize's pocketbook. The following is a digest of Thomas Walsh's translation and provides the context of the action in which the British army had the chance to demonstrate its mettle to the full:

- The army will attack tomorrow, so troops need to be in order of battle by 3:00 a.m. precisely, without beating of drums or other noise, and assembled 200 paces in front of the camp.
- The attack will commence at 4:30 a.m., an hour before daybreak.
- Reynier's division, the 13e and 85e Demi-Brigades, will extend its right towards the bridge on the canal of Alexandria.
- Friant will take position on the left of Reynier with the 25e, 61e and 75e Demi-Brigades.
- To the left of Friant, d'Estaing's column, comprising the 21e Demi-Brigade [Légère], and the grenadiers of the 25e and the Greeks, will act as an advance guard.
- Rampon, with the 3e Demi-Brigade and three companies of Carbiniers of the 2e Légère, will form the centre of the army with d'Estaing's column.
- Lanusse will take position to the left of Rampon with the 4e, 18e, 69e and 88e Demi-Brigades, extending his left to the sea.
- Thus: Reynier's and Friant's divisions form the right wing; d'Estaing's and Rampon's, the centre; and Lanusse's, the left wing. A light corps composed of Dromedaries and 30 cavalry, will advance on the enemy's left and make a false attack which will commence at the same time as the real attack. They will be under Reynier's orders.
- The rest of the cavalry will be posted to the rear of the centre and the

---

4   Aeneas Anderson, *Journal of the Forces under the Command of Sir Ralph Abercromby in the Mediterranean and Egypt* (London: J.Debrett 1802), p.252.

artillery of the reserve will take up a position behind the cavalry, with the foot guards behind them.

- The left wing under Lanusse's orders and the centre, under Rampon and d'Estaing, will begin the grand attack. They will advance upon the redoubts to their front and carry them with the bayonet.

- At the same time, the right wing under Reynier will refuse itself a little until the left is closely engaged. The centre will support the left wing as it moves briskly forward to attack and bear down on everything in front of it.

- After the enemy right and centre have been carried and the whole of his front line overthrown, the French army with the exception of the *tirailleurs* must quickly re-form and march against the second line.

- The left will begin the movement against the second line, refusing its right a little in order to outflank the enemy. The centre will then follow while the right wing will keep the enemy's left in check. The objective is to drive the enemy into Lake Maadieh.

- Roize, in command of the cavalry, will take advantage of any favourable circumstances to advance and cut down those of the enemy who have been shaken by the infantry attacks.

- Songis, in command of the artillery, will employ his guns to best advantage, but will also be aware of the gunboats on the flanks of his position. If necessary he will drive them off with 12-pounders. The generals commanding divisions will employ the artillery, whether battering or field pieces, as seems most suitable. The general commanding cavalry will do the same.

- The generals of division should form the head of their columns of attack, and their second line if they deem it necessary, in what they consider the most advantageous manner.

Before daybreak on the 21st, the sound of musketry was heard as the British troops were getting under arms. It seemed to be coming from the furthest fortification on the left, on the canal, where Cradock's brigade was posted. It was initially dismissed as a feint to test the readiness of the British troops, since it seemed to offer no material advantage. When the deeper tones of the guns came into play, it was obvious that something more serious was happening and Brigadier General Stuart in the second line prepared to move to the point of action. Indeed, the situation suddenly became critical when the French seized one of the fleches and turned the 12-pounder on the British troops. The guns in the redoubt responded and the French rapidly withdrew, taking with them three officers, a sergeant and ten rank and file as prisoners. They left behind an officer and four rank and file killed, but carried off their wounded.

Believing the British were fully occupied by this diversion on their left, and too precipitously according to one staff officer, the French commander in the field, *Général de Division* Lanusse, now prepared to attack the right with the main body of the army. Moore was general of the day on the 20th, and he had remained with the picquet of reserve through the night. There had been no sound from the French. Some rockets were fired, but this had happened too often to excite any concern. Moore now ordered the field officer of the picquet to retire to his post, and then rode along the line giving the same order to the other picquets. He had reached the left picquet of the Guards when he heard musket fire to the left where Cradock's brigade was posted. Everything was quiet on the right, though, and he assumed, as did everyone from Abercromby down, that it was a false alarm. As he was moving further left, however, he heard firing from the picquets of the Reserve. This convinced him the French were in earnest and he hurried back to the redoubt as the British picquets fell back. He then found the troops in the redoubt under strong attack.

The first French objective was to overthrow the Reserve, which they regarded as the most vulnerable part of the British line because of its advanced position. They would then be able to force the centre into retreat, at which point their cavalry would come into action to achieve the ultimate objective, which was of course to drive the whole British force into Lake Maadieh. The three-pronged attack now advancing on the British right, led over-all by Lanusse, comprised the columns of Rampon, who was to target the Guards and Coote's Brigade; Silly, with the redoubt as his objective; and Valentin, who by advancing along the shore would be in position to attack the troops posted in the ruins.

In contrast to the French estimation of their task, the right of the British line had strong defences which were manned by a considerable number of troops. These men had marched to the alarm posts at the first sound of musketry, and were supported by a strong battery. Stuart's Foreign Brigade was well placed to come up if necessary, while on the flank naval gunboats were able to come close enough inshore to enfilade any French advance, and did so under the highly efficient command of Captain Maitland RN. Furthermore, Moore and Oakes had already agreed that the redoubt and the ruins must be held at all cost. As a result of the general order which had the troops standing to arms an hour before daylight, the defenders there had fallen in before the attack began. Thus the 28th, under Colonel Paget, already had two companies in reserve to the left of the redoubt to guard the open rear, while the 58th lined the old ruins, which lay 20 to 30 yards behind the right flank of the redoubt. Oakes had led forward the left wing of the 42nd at the first intimations of the attack, while Moore sent orders to the right wing of the 23rd and the four flank companies of the 40th to position themselves in support of the 58th. In the half-light, though, it was difficult to discern what the French intended.

The French columns advance in their usual fashion, with impetuous bravery and noisy cries of *Vive la France! Vive la Republique!* They found themselves confronted by British discipline, steadiness and courage. Although Silly took a fleche and seized a gun, he was then driven back by fire from the redoubt, while fire from the ruins, defended by the 23rd, 58th and the four flank companies of the 40th, brought Valentin to a halt. Although checked, the French kept up a heavy fire with guns and muskets for about an hour. The 69e Demi-Brigade, which was leading the advance between the redoubt and the ruins, suffered such heavy fire from the 24-pounders, which were loaded with grape, that they were almost wiped out. The rest of the corps then refused to advance any further. Lanusse, trying to rally them, suffered a mortal wound.

Having failed to cross the ditch to his front, Silly now tried to turn the British position at the redoubt, supported by cavalry which swung round to the unprotected rear. At this point, Moore's horse was hit in the face, making him impossible to ride, and Paget was shot in the neck. Moore now realised that the French had turned the British left and were advancing towards the ruins. When he looked again he saw that the enemy columns were completely to the rear of the Reserve. The left wing of the 42nd had already arrived. When the right wing came up, Moore ordered the battalion to face about and drive the nearest French into the ruins, where they were killed, wounded, or forced to surrender. He then led them to the flank of the redoubt, where they attacked another French column. At this point Moore was shot in the leg, but he was able to report to Abercromby what had happened so far.

Unfortunately, the 42nd and the 28th pursued their opponents too far and suffered a sudden cavalry attack. This created considerable disorder, but the troops rallied and brought down so many men and horses that the remainder withdrew. Meanwhile, the 58th in the ruins let the French approach to within sixty yards and then fired a volley that brought them to a halt. However, the French cavalry were able to get behind the British and into the redoubt. They then came under fire from the 28th and were killed to a man. Meanwhile the 42nd were reduced to fighting individually as their numbers fell rapidly.

Abercromby, who was in the vicinity, was attacked in the midst of his own guard and nearly taken by a French dragoon. The cavalryman slashed at him but only inflicted a graze. He wheeled and attacked again, the lunge passing between Abercromby's side and his right arm, which he clamped to retain the sabre. The dragoon was then shot by a man in the 42nd. Moore also came under attack. He galloped clear and then rode into the ruins to bring up the troops that were there and whom he found in good order. He ordered the 40th to fire a couple of volleys from the ruins which saw off yet more of the French. By this time Stuart had brought up his foreign battalions, who were sharing in the action and behaving with admirable spirit. Thus every French attack on the Reserve was seen off with great slaughter. When ammunition ran dangerously low, Moore brought as many men as possible into the redoubt to protect them from the galling French fire. Even when they were completely without ammunition, the French seemed too bruised to renew the attack, although the cavalry took advantage of the guns falling silent. They attacked the batteries, slashing in all directions, with the result that 60 artillerymen were killed or wounded. One battery was completely overrun and, according to the sergeant in command, they would have been killed to the last man had not the 42nd come to their rescue. Once ammunition had been brought up from the depot, though, the French drew back under renewed fire.

While the Reserve had been struggling to hold its ground, *Général de Division* Rampon was pushing his attack on the Guards and Coote's Brigades, where the 92nd had just come into position on the left. They had actually commenced their march to Aboukir before daybreak but had marched only a short distance when they heard the sound of musketry on the left and an order from Abercromby brought them to a halt. He mounted his horse, which as always was already saddled, and rode over to see what was happening. By this time the 92nd could not only see the flash of every pan but could also hear the roar of gunfire accompanied by the sound of more concentrated musketry. To a man they were eager to join the fight, but when the sound died down, Abercromby decided it was a false alarm. He ordered them to continue their march. They had advanced only a few paces when they heard firing on the right. At once there were loud calls from the ranks that they should be allowed to take their place in the line. Major Napier, in command, consulted with Abercromby, who acceded to the men's eagerness.

The order was given to turn about and march back to their former position on the left of Coote's Brigade. They struggled into their place because the 2/1st and the 54th were closing into the centre as they prepared to advance. It was still not light enough to see who was doing exactly what, and they could only wait until such time as the firing erupted in front of them. Nevertheless, every man realised the French were making a powerful and determined attack. Once formed, they heard the French *pas de charge,* at which Napier ordered them to stay put because they were on rising ground. He desired them to remain cool and steady, and fire with as much precision as possible. In response, they held fire for as long as possible and then poured a devastating volley into the French ranks. The enemy continued to advance, however, so the 92nd, having been ordered to stand fast and defend themselves to the last, prepared to receive the enemy with the bayonet. The French advance became more hesitant but they strengthened it with two guns loaded with grape, which did dreadful execution on the British ranks. The order was given to lie down and skirmishers were thrown forward from all the battalions in the brigade. The cannonade continued until one of the guns exploded and the soldiers saw the gunners blown into the air. The other gun was then withdrawn and the French infantry was also pulled back under cavalry cover.

This account, from two men in the ranks of the 92nd, overlaps with what had been happening to their right, where Rampon tried to turn the left of the Guards. It was a fierce struggle, fought in smoke so dense that only the flashes from the muskets penetrated it. Eventually, brisk fire from the 3rd Foot Guards, whose left was thrown back, and from the 2/1st, supported on the left by the newly arrived 92nd, caused the French to recoil. Although they recovered and returned fire, they were finally forced to withdraw after a sharp contest. They were then sent on their way by the British gunners, who were using lanterns so that they could see to load.

Meanwhile, *Général de Brigade* Destaing had managed to penetrate the British lines by way of the hollow formed by the road from Aboukir to Alexandria. Leaving the redoubt on his left, he headed for the ruins. Here he encountered the 42nd, who counter-attacked with the bayonet. His leading unit, the 21e Légère, had advanced too far and when they tried to withdraw they were surrounded and forced to surrender.

The French infantry now withdrew, having failed at all points. Menou, desperate and determined to win the day, ordered *Général de Brigade* Roize to charge the British lines. The infantry, led by *Général de Division* Reynier, with Lanusse's, Rampon's and Friant's divisions, plus the 85e demi-brigade, were to provide support. It was later learnt the Roize had twice remonstrated with Menou because he recognised that to carry out the order would be suicidal. He finally obeyed at the third time of telling, and died as a result. Leading the charge were the 3e and 14e Dragons under *Général de Brigade* Boussart, who galloped through the 42nd at the redoubt and reached as far as the British tents. Some of the horsemen were then brought down because they stumbled into the dips the 28th had dug as sleep holes. Others became entangled with in the tent ropes. There was a suspicion amongst the British that they were under the influence of strong liquor because they fell from the saddle as they wielded their sabres. Behind them came the 15e, 18e and 2e Dragons, led by Roize. The Minorca Regiment had already come to the support of the 42nd, which had been ordered by Colonel Brent Spencer to wheel about to the left so that they flanked the cavalry. This enabled them to recover and attack with great spirit as the French cavalry sounded the retreat. The 28th famously opened ranks to let the cavalry gallop through, then turned about and discharged such volleys as brought down large numbers of men and horses. Roize died at this point and the cavalry retreated in disorder.

It was during this stage of the battle that Anton Lutz, a private in the Minorca Regiment, seized the standard of the 21e Légère, which boasted of the unit's victories in Italy. This standard had first been taken by Sergeant Sinclair of the 42nd, but had been lost during the cavalry charges. Later, Lutz received twenty dollars and a certificate from the adjutant general, and might have expected promotion, but his illiteracy made it impossible. Sinclair was eventually rewarded with a commission.

When some of the supporting French infantry seized a small outwork about 100 yards from the redoubt and turned the guns on the redoubt, the grenadiers of the 40th attacked and retook it. They were then able to turn the guns on another advancing French column.

All this while and British left and the French right had been skirmishing and exchanging gunfire, but neither side had made any attempt to turn the contest into something more serious. The British lacked the means; the French lacked the intention. The second line, which with the exception of Stuart's brigade had seen little of the action, still suffered casualties, particularly as the battle drew to a close. The French, still drawn up in battle order, treated the British to a final cannonade. Because of the elevation of the guns, their targets were the troops of the second line rather than the first. The British gunners immediately responded and caused losses to their opponents, who seemed uncertain what to do next. When two ammunition waggons exploded, the enemy fire finally slackened. At about 9:30 a.m. the French began to withdraw. By 10:00 a.m. all firing had ceased and the French were able to extricate themselves unhindered by any pursuit thanks to their opponents' lack of cavalry.

Thus ended what a staff officer described as a glorious and ever memorable action. But there was a price to pay. The French losses were much the heavier, estimated at about 5,000, including three generals killed (Lanusse, Roize, and Baudot) and two wounded (Destaing, Silly), while 250 men were taken prisoner. The British lost 1,464, killed, wounded and missing out of a total strength of just under 12,000. Generals Moore, Hope, Oakes and Lawson were all wounded, as was Sir Sidney Smith, but the greatest loss was Sir Ralph Abercromby. Although the wound he received from the French dragoon had been superficial, he had also taken a shot to the thigh. When he was urged to have the wound attended to, he refused because he believed his absence would distress the troops. Instead, he concealed it from all but a trusted few until he was on the point of fainting, by which time the battle had been won. If there was anything that demonstrated the affection of the troops for their commander, it was their response as he was carried past them by a party from the 92nd. As Robertson of the 92nd remembered, when they knew their respected commander was dangerously wounded, the interest excited was so great that everyone ran to get a sight of him whom they all loved.

> British Losses:
> Killed: 10 officers, 9 sergeants, 224 rank and file, 2 horses
> Wounded: 60 officers (6 later returned 'since dead'), 48 sergeants, 3 drummers, 1032 rank and file, 3 horses
> Missing: 3 officers, 1 sergeant, 28 rank and file

Baird's Advance on Cairo

Major General David Baird set sail from Bombay for the Red Sea on the 6 April with about 7,500 men, two thirds of them sepoys, one third European troops. The mood was exultant. As James McGrigor, the surgeon of the 88th, commented in his journal, there was universal joy, for fighting and promotion were considered the certain results of an expedition to that quarter of the world. The voyage proved difficult, however. The ships were dispersed by gales, and the Red Sea was particularly challenging to navigate, with the result that when Baird reached Mocha on 25 April he discovered that part of the fleet, carrying half his force, had sailed on to Jeddah and other ships were unaccounted for. When another contingent reached Mocha on the 28 April, Baird sailed with them to Jeddah, where he arrived on 17 May. At the same time, he sent some of his troops to Kosseir to establish the British position there. In Jeddah Baird learnt that troops he had expected to find there had set sail for Suez, while there was no news of yet another contingent. At this point the men from the Cape of Good Hope joined the force from India.

On 8 June Baird himself reached Kosseir, which he had now appointed as his rendezvous, to find that the two divisions he had assumed to be at Suez had been waiting at Kosseir for six weeks. He now had nearly 6,000 troops, although a quarter of his force was still missing. A week after his arrival he received a dispatch from Hely-Hutchinson, brought by Rear Admiral Blankett from Suez, where Hely-Hutchinson had assumed the troops from India to be. The message informed him that the commander-in-chief would remain near Cairo until the Indian force had crossed the desert and reached the Nile, after which they could travel on by boat, aided by the river being in flood.

Meanwhile, the first British troops had long since landed at Suez. On the 21 April HMS *Leopard*, flying Rear Admiral Blankett's flag had reached Suez accompanied by a few frigates, sloops and transports, and had landed the 86th Foot. There had been no opposition because the French garrison had already evacuated the town. On the 7 June, while Baird was at still at Kosseir, Colonel Lloyd responded to an order from Hely-Hutchinson and set out with about 200 men of the 86th to march to Cairo, a distance of about sixty miles. Because Blankett had been cruising in the Red Sea to protect the route to India since Bonaparte's arrival in Egypt, neither he nor Lloyd had any idea of Baird's whereabouts, hence Lloyd's decision to wait only for some promised camels to arrive and then to make for Cairo as Hely-Hutchinson required. His four-day march was in sharp contrast to the difficulties faced by Baird's force. Nevertheless, by the battalion's own account, it was a gruelling experience during which three officers and twenty men either died of thirst or perished in the desert when they were too weak to keep up. The officers had to throw away some of their baggage to preserve the strength of the camels, and the men abandoned their knapsacks. As Lord Dalhousie cynically commented, however, it was only gruelling when compared with the luxury of an Indian advance, when the baggage train would have dwarfed the detachment of soldiers – Lloyd was reported to have had dozens of shirts and innumerable bottles of Madeira wine in his *light* baggage.

Earlier in the year the next stage for Baird would have been to sail on to Suez and take advantage of the established route to Cairo. At this time of year, though, the winds were consistently northerly, so he decided instead to advance from Kosseir to Kenneh and the Nile, using an old, much decayed trade route. This would be a potentially dangerous march of over 100 miles, and he realised he needed to devise a strategy that would keep the troops alive in the desolate and deserted landscape that they now needed to traverse, across terrain that varied from loose sand and scree to rocky ravines. All the while the sun at the height of its summer power would beat down on them, and then there was the question of water. There were said to be wells on the route, but their precise location was not known. Indeed, it transpired that some of them were thirty miles apart. This was normally a three-day march in desert conditions but the troops would not be able to continue for three days without water.

One vital element of Baird's planning, after he had ordered that women, children, and the sick should remain at Kosseir, was to send his army forward in small detachments, which would march only at night, spend the day under canvas, and be able to leave food and water in place for the detachment that followed them. Water, mixed with vinegar to counteract the brackishness, was carried in skin bags or wooden casks loaded on camels and then distributed at the rate of two gallons a man. This was supplemented by half a pint of wine and rice water, which was drunk at the commencement of each march. The camels also proved useful for carrying those who fell sick or went lame during the march. Other beasts that supported the advance were the bullocks that hauled the guns and carried the baggage. As a further means towards a minimalist approach the men were ordered by their officers to throw away any unnecessary possessions, so that they were left with just shirts and shoes.

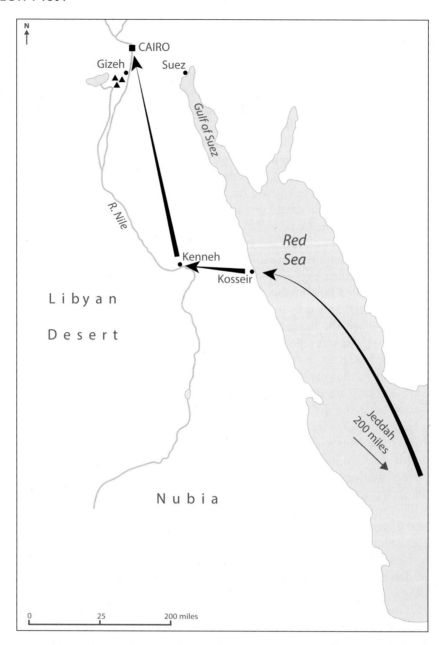

Baird's advance on Cairo.

The sepoys, who were assumed to be better able to cope with the conditions, carried their own accoutrements and yet, in the event, it was the Indians who suffered the most, two of them even being driven to commit suicide.

On 19 June the first detachments set off for Kenneh. For one of the soldiers who had come up from the verdure of the Cape it was an advance through a dreadful dreary desert, over hills, rocks and mountains, through valleys and across plains of sand, the sand itself so hot that it seemed like walking through fire. Neither grass nor water was to be seen and desperate men put pebbles in their mouth to create some fluid. Yet, as Baird himself wrote in a general order issued after his return to India, no-one could have failed to be impressed by the cheerful mood and persevering efforts of the troops throughout their laborious march.

Baird himself reached Kenneh on 8 July. Here he halted, awaiting further orders from Hely-Hutchinson. None came, and he began to contemplate returning to the Red Sea and carrying out the further orders he had received, to attack Mauritius or the Dutch East Indies. When he learnt from the aide he had sent to Cairo to discover what was happening there that the city had fallen, his mind was made up and he prepared for a return march to Kosseir. Before he could depart, however, he received a letter from Hely-Hutchinson instructing him to advance on Gizeh. Once all his troops had reached Kenneh, the whole force sailed down the Nile in germes. At Gizeh, there were further orders. The advance was to continue to Rosetta. Baird's army finally arrived there on 31 August, a day before the formal surrender of Alexandria.

Yet, although Baird's troops had met nothing but hardship and frustration, back in Britain the advance from Kosseir to Kenneh caught the public imagination and became the stuff of legend, to the point where it was claimed that the only casualty on that dreadful march was a drummer boy. In fact, the total casualties were a paymaster and twelve men, who died of sunstroke, while the 8th Light Dragoons lost some of their horses; but this is still a telling comment on the efficacy of Baird's arrangements and the spirit of his men.

7

A Greatly Lamented Death

Although it was Major General Hely-Hutchinson who brought about the final departure of the French from Egypt and subsequently received the thanks of both Houses, for those who had been part of the campaign and for men back in Britain like the King, the Duke of York and Henry Dundas, now ex-Minister for War after Pitt's resignation, there could be no doubt to whom the success properly belonged. Lieutenant General Sir Ralph Abercromby was not just the hero of the hour as the early stages of the campaign demonstrated the prowess of this new British army; he was also a man who had earned the deepest affection of the men who served under him or worked with him.

Hely-Hutchinson himself, in his official dispatch of 5 April, wrote that the army had

> sustained an irreparable loss in the person of our never sufficiently to be lamented Commander in Chief… I believe he was wounded early, but he concealed his situation from those about him, and continued in the field, giving his orders with that coolness and perspicuity, which have ever marked his character, till long after the action was over, when he fainted though weakness of blood. Were it permitted for a soldier to regret any one who has fallen in the service of his country, I might be excused for lamenting him, more than any other person; but it is some consolation to those who tenderly loved him, that as his life was honourable, so was his death glorious. His memory will be recorded in the annals of his country – will be sacred to every British soldier – and embalmed in the recollection of a grateful prosperity.[1]

Captain Thomas Walsh of the 93rd paid homage in his journal to the memory of the man who had led a British army to victory, a man whose death in action was probably inevitable, sooner or later, because of his style of command. Not for him command from a distance, however wise this might have been for a commander-in-chief: for him there was no other place but in the thick of the fighting with his troops, many of whom were still learning their business. And they loved him for it.

---

1   Walsh, *Journal*, Appendix No.6, pp.26-27.

The death of Abercromby.
(Anne S.K. Brown Military
Collection)

Walsh's entry for 29 March conveys something of his feelings when he received

… the melancholy tidings of Sir Ralph Abercromby's decease. At eleven the preceding night death snatched form us this beloved commander. The wound which he received on the 21st, bringing on fever and mortification, occasioned this lamented event, and our most valiant general was lost to us at the moment when we stood most in need of his assistance. The ball had entered the thigh very high up, and taking a direction towards the groin, had lodged in the bone, whence it could not be extracted.

In the action of the 13th March, he had suffered a contusion of the thigh from a musket ball, and had a horse killed under him. On the 21st, at the time when he received his death wound, he was in the very midst of the enemy, and personally engaged with an officer of dragoons, who was at that moment shot by a corporal of the forty-second. Sir Ralph retained the officer's sword, which had passed between his arm and his side the instant before the officer fell.

During the seven days, which elapsed from the period of his being wounded till his death, the anguish and torture he endured must have been extreme. Yet not a groan, not a complaint escaped his lips, and he continued to the last a bright example of patience and fortitude. He thought and talked of nothing else to all around him, but the bravery and heroic conduct of the army, which he said he could not sufficiently admire.

A man who has served his country in every quarter of the globe; who, as a commander, devotes to his troops an attention almost parental; as a soldier, shares in all their hardships and all their dangers; who, at an age when he might retire from the field crowned with glory, comes forth, at the call of his country, a veteran in experience, youthful in ardour; whose life is a public blessing, his death a universal misfortune; is beyond the hacknied phrase of panegyric. Such a man was Sir Ralph Abercromby. Dead to his country, his name will ever live in her recollection. Through his exertions, seconded by the cooperation of those he commanded, a nation, long oppressed in a sanguinary war, caught the first glimpse of an honourable *peace*.[2]

For Moore, who had served with Abercromby in the West Indies, Ireland and North Holland, the loss was more personal. In his journal he wrote:

Sir Ralph was a truly upright, honourable, judicious man; his great sagacity, which had been pointed all his life to military matters, made him an excellent officer... It was impossible, knowing him as I did, not to have the greatest respect and friendship for him; he had ever treated me with marked kindness. The only consolation I feel is, that his death has been nearly that which he himself wished, that his country, grateful to his memory, will hand down his name to posterity with the admiration it deserves.

Moore went on to tell his family that:

Sir Ralph has fallen at a moment most unfortunate for his country. We stand in need of his experience, his sagacity, and judgement to extricate us; but he could have fallen at no moment more fortunately for his own fame. It has happened to no other General during the war to beat the French in three successive actions. He will be honoured and lamented by his country, and his name handed down to posterity with the most distinguished of his countrymen. This is the consolation I derive from the loss of the best man, and best soldier, who has appeared amongst us this war.[3]

On 29 April Abercromby was given a military funeral before burial at St John's Bastion, Fort St Elmo, Malta. His grave was marked with a slab of black marble, on which was engraved an epitaph which praised him both for his integrity, magnanimity and military prowess and for his fidelity to his king and country. He was, as Henry Bunbury later wrote, 'a gentleman', with all that word implied to his contemporaries.

2   Walsh, *Journal*, pp.110-112.
3   Moore, *Diary*, Vol.II, pp.18-19

8

Medical Services

When the Medical Board made arrangements for the medical services that would support the expedition to Egypt, they appointed the physician Dr James Franck as principal medical officer. Franck had served in Lisbon, and had been with Stuart when Corsica was taken in 1794, and it was Stuart's recommendation that led to his appointment as head of the medical services in the Mediterranean. Since he was on the spot, he was the natural choice when Egypt became the objective. In January 1801, however, Franck was replaced by Inspector General of Hospitals, Thomas Young, seemingly at General Abercromby's instigation. Franck remained with the expedition in the more subsidiary role of inspector, and was responsible for setting up the first plague hospital at Aboukir. He would later serve under Wellington in the Peninsula, but without the diligence that the post required.

There is no record of how Franck got on with Abercromby when the latter replaced Stuart as commander of the army in the Mediterranean, or even whether Abercromby had any reservations about Franck's capabilities. He may merely have felt that a surgeon was preferable to a physician as head of the medical services. It is certain, however, that Abercromby had established a good working relationship with Young in the West Indies during an expedition where careful attention had been given to the provision of appropriate medical personnel, supplies, and equipment.

Young had considerable experience as a military surgeon, having served with the 1/1st (Royals) and then as surgeon to the Grenada garrison. He saw further service in Flanders (1793-1795), and after his second period in the West Indies he accompanied the Anglo-Russian expedition to North Holland (1799). This experience certainly made him better equipped than Franck to perform the duties of principal medical officer on active service. He was not popular with the Medical Board, however, and was particularly disliked by the Surgeon General, Thomas Keate. This went back to Young's second period in the West Indies. Keate reserved for himself and the Medical Board the right to fill vacancies which occurred during a campaign. Young, though, had insisted upon promoting the men he thought best qualified, men who were in the West Indies and understood the problems peculiar to the Caribbean. In this he enjoyed Abercromby's support, presumably because the general recognised that a man with experience of conditions in the Caribbean was preferable to someone sent out from Britain. To the Medical Board, though, it seemed that Young was given to favouritism.

Young joined the Egypt expedition at Marmaris Bay, to be confronted by over 1,000 sick troops, over a tenth of the expeditionary force. This was the result of the men's confinement on board insalubrious transports; although the rotations of the battalions to spend time ashore while their ships were fumigated was already having a positive effect. The sick from all ships were now brought ashore to aid their recovery. In other respects, though, Young found sufficient medical staff, equipment and supplies to satisfy his exacting standards. These resources included the manpower to establish a general hospital. In addition, depots had been set up at Malta and Gibraltar, so that he had access to further supplies. This thoroughness, emanating from the Medical Board, was evidence that lessons had been learnt since 1793.

The first medical challenge, other than the permanent problem of sickness, was the landings at Aboukir, where casualties were inevitable. Arrangements were made for the sick already on naval ships to be cared for by naval surgeons. The sick on the transports were transferred to one mother-ship, to be tended by assistant surgeons, aided by convalescent soldiers and some soldiers' wives as orderlies and nurses. Fifteen transports had been converted into hospital ships, ready to receive the wounded, and there were another two at Rhodes.

Once the landings commenced, naval boats would be on standby to evacuate the wounded from the beach. Regimental surgeons were directed to accompany their battalions into action and establish temporary dressing stations as quickly as possible. Staff surgeons would land as soon as the beach was secured. Young would direct operations from HMS *Niger*, while Franck was on one of the hospital ships, *Harmony*.

These arrangements were summed up in a general order that indicates how much Abercromby and Young had learnt from the chaos of the landings in North Holland.

A proportion of the general medical staff must be attached in the first instance to each brigade, and will be allowed such orderlies as are necessary from each brigade. Regimental surgeons are to be allowed one orderly each to carry the field case of instruments. When any wounded are brought down to the beach and a request shall be made for their being conveyed on board the hospital ship the captain of the division to whom such application shall be made is to direct some of the boats under his orders to perform this service, and, if necessary, that the flat boats shall be removed that the soldiers may be placed with convenience and ease themselves, directing cutters and other boats to tow them. This service is particularly directed to the attention of Captain Apthorpe whose division is attached to the Medical Department. After the troops are on shore the stores belonging to the general hospital are to be landed.[1]

1   Lt.Gen. Sir Neil Cantlie, *A History of the Army Medical Department* (London: Longmans Group Ltd, 1973), pp.265, 267.

In these landings, of course, the regimental surgeons shared the danger of the soldiers, and it was inevitable that there would be casualties among the medical men. The Coldstreamers lost their surgeon, George Rose, during the action, and two surgeons were wounded.

As the army advanced towards Alexandria, another problem appeared, the difficulty of moving wounded soldiers, like those of 13 March at Mandorah, across difficult terrain. Fortunately, the discovery that Lake Maadieh was navigable for naval boats provided an easy solution. Later, when part of the army was advancing towards Cairo, the Nile was used for evacuation purposes.

A far more intractable problem was caused by the nature of the country. Heat, dust, flies, and the general lack of basic hygiene meant that bowel problems such as enteritis and dysentery became increasingly common and were often exacerbated by contaminated water. By 14 March Young was trying to cope with about 2,400 sick, while a further 1,000 had already been sent to stations in the Mediterranean. In desperation, he called in both medical personnel and supplies from Minorca. He also demanded, in the peremptory manner which he so often adopted, that the Medical Board should send out more hospital mates and stores. The Board, recognising necessity, and no doubt swallowing their collective annoyance, gave Young what he had requested. At the same time, realising that facilities at Aboukir were overstretched, Young set up a second general hospital near Alexandria. Even so, the number of sick, not counting the wounded, continued to rise inexorably. By the end March a quarter of the force was out of action.

Not surprisingly, this high incidence continued during the advance on Cairo, when temperatures reached 49°C (120°F). Although another general hospital was established in Rosetta, the insanitary conditions of the town made hygiene difficult to maintain.

By this time, two of Egypt's other endemic conditions had made themselves felt: bubonic plague and ophthalmia. Yet another general hospital was set up to deal with the rising sick list and a staff surgeon, John Webb, appointed inspector of field hospitals. Nor was Keate remiss in performing his obligations to the campaign. Appreciating the problems Young faced, he sent out Inspector of Hospitals, Dr Shapter, and an additional surgeon, physician, and apothecary, three hospital mates, a purveyor's clerk, and extra supplies and equipment.

Taken over all, it may be said that Young justified Abercromby's preference for a surgeon experienced in campaign conditions. He continued the high-handed approach to appointments that he had used the West Indies, and which had earned him the disfavour of the Medical Board; but his defence, that it was better to fill vacancies with men whose competence he had witnessed than with unknown personnel from Britain, was justified by the efficiency with which the medical aspects of the campaign were conducted. In the most difficult conditions of a country where good hygiene was virtually unknown and endemic diseases quickly spread through the ranks, Young did at least ensure that the sick would receive the best care possible.

Bubonic Plague and Ophthalmia

Although most of the fatalities during the campaign were the result of dysentery, this was a condition with which most surgeons were familiar. Few of them, though, had any experience of treating patients suffering from the plague or ophthalmia. Between April and the beginning of August 1801 there were 380 cases of plague receiving treatment at Rosetta and Aboukir, of whom 173 died. The doctors recognised that they were dealing with a contagious condition, even if they did not fully understand its cause. It was noted, for example, that when a battalion moved on, the problem disappeared: this was because the fleas carrying the infection did not travel with them. To prevent the spread of the plague, strict quarantine conditions were enforced and armed sentries guarded the hospital tents. As a further precaution against the spread of the disease from Aboukir, where it first broke out, Major General Coote set up a line of sentries and vedettes across the peninsula at the Mandorah redoubt, so that no-one could pass without written permission. Furthermore, strict cleanliness was observed in camp.

Treatment consisted of doses of calomel, opium, and nitric acid, mercurial ointment, and the immersion of hands and feet in a nitric bath. The dedication of the medical men is also noted in several journals. One of them, Doctor Allen, himself succumbed to the disease as the result at the care and zeal with which he treated his patients.

More serious for its long-term consequences, although not of itself a fatal condition, was ophthalmia, also known as trachmia or Egyptian ophthalmia. This was an infection of the eyes caused by the bacterium *chlamydia trachomatis*. It was endemic in Egypt, and could be observed in every town and village to the point that is was rare to see people who were not affected. Even the women, whose eyes were the only visible part of their face, were marked by it. No British army had previously encountered the condition, which was a challenge for the medical men. Furthermore, it spread with frightening speed through the army. As with the enteric diseases, the generally insanitary conditions and the presence of swarms of flies undoubtedly increased the incidence of the infection. There was also the belief that the glare of the sun was partly responsible. Because the condition first appeared in the French army after the Battle of Alexandria, the distinguished French surgeon, Dominique Jean Larrey, concluded that the exertion of fighting, the coldness of the night, and the mist from the nearby lake were all contributory factors. Only with the wisdom of hindsight did British surgeons finally conclude that it was a contagious condition spread either by touch or by the sharing of washing water and towels.

The condition first became evident in a sufferer as purulent conjunctivitis. In the most severe cases this would develop into panophthalmitis, suppuration, and serious affection of the eyeball. The risk was that the breakdown of the cornea would bring about blindness.

It was observed that it was often the most fit and active men who suffered, from which the seemingly logical conclusion was drawn that they must be weakened by venesection, by which anything from twenty to as much as sixty ounces of blood were withdrawn. They were also banned from eating meat.

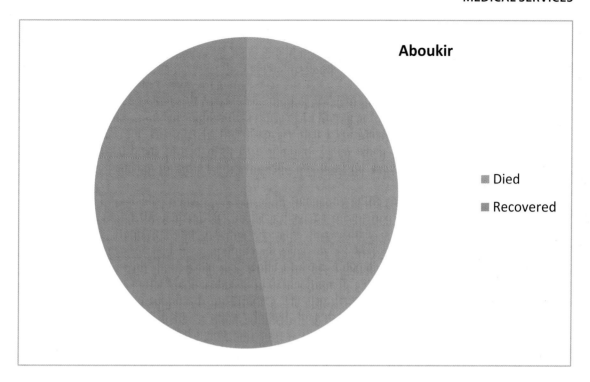

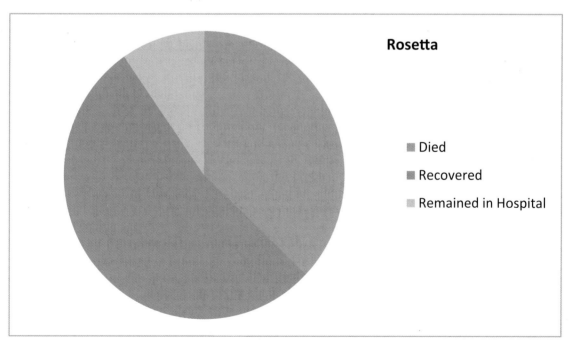

Bubonic Plague Recovery Rates, Aboukir and Rosetta.
Data from 'Return of Patients affected by the Plague, received into the General Hospitals at Aboukir and Rosetta, during the Months of April, May, June, July and August, 1801', signed by Thomas Young, Inspector-General, reproduced in in Walsh, *Journal*, p.41.

Various drugs were prescribed such as mercury and antimony, and there was localised application of sulphate of copper and other powerful substances. In extreme cases there was surgical intervention, but since the implements were unsterilized, this did more harm than good. Interestingly, the French surgeons confined their treatment to scarification of the patient's temples and eyelids, which seems to have been markedly more effective, presumably on the basis that for this condition too much intervention was self-defeating.

By the end of the campaign, 160 men were totally blind, while a further 200 had lost the sight of one eye. Indeed, the 50th Foot became known as the 'Blind Half Hundred', because they suffered so severely. This was only the beginning, though. The highly contagious nature of ophthalmia meant that units which had fought in Egypt carried it to wherever British soldiers were subsequently stationed. Indeed, it became one of the most frequent reasons for discharge, as the casualty returns of the period attest. This in turn led to the suspicion, strongly held by some surgeons, that it was often self-inflicted in order to escape from the army *and* gain a pension. Meanwhile, the French soldier was spreading it as assiduously as the British, so that by the end of the Napoleonic Wars there was scarcely a European army that was not affected.

On a more positive note, in August 1800 the army started a programme of vaccination against smallpox, using Edward Jenner's method. This was initially carried out in a somewhat haphazard fashion because many generals opposed its use on their troops. In Egypt, however, a more thorough approach was adopted because it was rightly anticipated that there was a high risk of a smallpox epidemic in that country. Two civilian doctors joined the army in 1801 and vaccinated the whole force. They also offered vaccination to any Turks who also wished to be inoculated. Thus one of the scourges that might have afflicted the army was avoided.

In conclusion, despite operating in a country where insanitary conditions were the norm, acerbated by heat, dust, and the prevalence of flies, the medical services proved as efficient as contemporary knowledge allowed. The mismanagement of the Flanders campaign and the inadequacies suffered by the expedition to North Holland were avoided, and much of the credit must belong to Thomas Young, difficult character though he was, and all the other medical personnel who willingly put their own lives at risk, whether on the beach at Aboukir or in the plague hospitals, to keep the troops alive and in health.

9

A Wasted Army?

A Definitive Peace?

The Treaty of Amiens was signed in March 1802, while some of the British troops were still in Egypt. Some kind of peace had been under discussion since 1799, but Pitt's government, particularly its foreign secretary, Lord Grenville, had suspected Bonaparte of simply playing for time so that he could build up his power base and increase his military and naval capacity. Pitt's resignation on 14 March 1801, over the king's refusal to sanction Catholic emancipation, led to a new government led by Henry Addington. He realised that the country was war weary and, perhaps having a more naïve opinion of Bonaparte than Grenville, began to sound out the possibility of peace. As a result, a preliminary agreement was signed on 30 September 1801, just a month after Menou capitulated in Alexandria.

This agreement stated in principal that Britain would surrender most of the possessions taken from the French and abandon the ports she occupied in the Mediterranean, while the French would return Egypt to the Ottomans and withdraw from most of Italy. Britain would retain Ceylon from the Dutch and, by secret agreement, hold on to Trinidad and Tobago, which had been taken from the Spanish.

The promise of peace was greeted in Britain with wild enthusiasm, including public demonstrations and firework displays, based on the belief that it would ease the hardship suffered by so much of the population. Yet those of a more cynical disposition soon realised that the British government's need to sign a peace treaty gave Bonaparte the whip hand. As a result the British negotiator, the Marquis Cornwallis, quickly grasped that his opposite numbers, Talleyrand and Joseph Bonaparte, were playing a slippery game that left him at a permanent disadvantage. Then there were the Dutch, side-lined by the French as a vassal state, and the Spanish, unaware of what was being arranged on their behalf.

Bonaparte's double-dealing became clear when in January 1802 he accepted the presidency of the Italian Republic, a collection of northern Italian states which had been taken from the Austrians. This negated one of the terms of the Treaty of Lunéville which bound the French to respect Italian independence.

As the negotiations continued, it soon became clear that the principal stumbling block was Malta, with the defences that Abercromby had so convincingly recommended to the government should remain in British hands. It was finally decided that the island should be returned to the Knights of St John but how this was to be achieved when Bonaparte had dissolved the order remained unresolved. Similarly, the extra condition, that the island's neutrality should be guaranteed by some neutral powers, was agreed without any such powers being identified. Addington, however, was under public pressure to sign what was to be called a *Definitive Treaty of Peace*. Furthermore, he was about to present his budget to Parliament. Cornwallis, therefore, was instructed to sign an agreement as long as it fell short of something the British people would not accept. As a result, the Peace of Amiens was finally signed on 25 March 1802.

The terms were similar to the preliminary agreement but it was now out in the open that Spain would not regain Trinidad and Tobago, nor their long-held objective, Gibraltar, although Britain was to return Minorca to them and also to evacuate Elba. As for the Dutch, so completely had they been excluded that Cornwallis engineered a separate agreement with them that returned most of Dutch Guiana and the Cape of Good Hope, although not Ceylon. It was further agreed between the British and French, that the former would withdraw troops from Egypt and the latter would do the same in the Papal States and Naples. As for Malta, Britain would leave within three months of signing the treaty and Russia would become the Order's protector.

Perhaps the playwright and Member of Parliament, Richard Brinsley Sheridan, summed up the attitude of those who saw little to celebrate in this peace. It was, he told the Whig grandee Lord Holland, a peace which one ought to be glad of but no man could be proud of. Sheridan had once been an uncritical admirer of Bonaparte, but that admiration was running thin as Bonaparte himself revealed his greed for power. Although it was Britain who finally declared war in May 1803, Napoleon's overt exercise of French dominance in Europe, particularly in Switzerland and the German states, and his blatant moves to strengthen his navy and build up his army reserves, certainly went against the spirit of Amiens. He also made clear that there was no role for Britain in Europe and the Mediterranean. War was inevitable: if not Britain, then there can be little doubt that the First Consul would have engineered an excuse to break the treaty. After all, Britain had yet to evacuate Malta.

The Army of Egypt

As has already been demonstrated, the army that Abercromby took to Egypt was the best that Britain had put into the field in eight years of war, and the first to really test the mettle of the French. This was the result of the careful nurturing that for some of the troops had started in North Holland, or even the West Indies. It then continued on Minorca and during the vital weeks of preparation and practice at Marmaris Bay. Once peace had been re-established, however, it was inevitable that the Army of Egypt would be dispersed. By

1803, when war broke out again, sixteen of the infantry battalions and two of the cavalry units were back on home service. Hompesch's Mounted Riflemen had been disbanded, and the 26th Light Dragoons had been renumbered as the 23rd. In theory, home service meant anywhere in the British Isles. In practice, most of them would be in Ireland. Mainland Britain did not like the presence of soldiers; the Irish just had to put up with it.

The 2/1st joined their senior battalion in the West Indies. Three of the Egypt battalions were serving in the Gibraltar garrison, three more were in Sicily, including two of the foreign regiments. Stuart's Minorcans were sent to Britain. Two battalions were still in Malta, evidence that Britain had indeed broken the terms of the treaty. All the Indian troops returned to their native country, along with two British battalions (the 88th were on Home service) and Baird's only cavalry unit, the 8th Light Dragoons, who went to India rather then returning to the Cape. One of Baird's original battalions, the 10th, remained in Egypt before moving on to Malta, and one was described simply as serving in the Mediterranean. It was not until Britain became thoroughly engaged in the Iberian Peninsula that the need for a considerable concentration of troops became a crucial requirement. With so many units scattered around the globe, however, it proved increasingly necessary to call upon the second battalions that were hastily raised once the war had resumed.

At the end of a period of conflict, with the signing of treaties that are meant to endure, British governments have all too often fallen for the promise of peace and used it as a justification for cutting military expenditure. To be fair to Addington, he applied the shears rather more sparingly than some of his predecessors. He still cut, though. All the regiments numbered over 95 were disbanded (The 95th was actually raised in 1802 as an experimental rifle corps). Furthermore, most of the second battalions were also disbanded, so that in 1803 the 1st and the 54th were the only regiments with two battalions. The 60th (Royal Americans) had six, but they were all in the West Indies at this point. The lost battalions, it will be remembered, had often taken in volunteers from the Militia to make up their numbers. These independent-minded men, as Abercromby described them, could with the right care and attention be turned into excellent soldiers. Some of them came back through Addington's desperate measure to make good his shearing, the Army of Reserve, but many of them were lost to the army.

Many of the regiments which had served in Egypt later served in the Peninsula, often in the form of their second battalions. It cannot be demonstrated for certain how many of them remembered the lessons Abercromby had taught. Yet there were certainly many who still recalled the glory days of 1801, and for those who had forgotten or had never experienced them, there were men in senior command to remind them. Moore commented that Abercromby's weakness was his extreme short-sightedness. For that reason he needed good executive senior officers who would be able to implement the orders they were given. One only needs to mention the names of John Hope, George Murray, and Moore himself to realise that 'Abercromby's pupils', as Thomas Picton called them (including himself in this description), were prominent in the forces that fought in Spain and Portugal.

Colonel Thomas Graham arrived in Egypt to take command of his regiment, the 90th, just after Hely-Hutchinson had received the surrender of Belliard at Cairo. Despite this disappointment, he remained for the rest of the campaign, and later wrote that the troops had finally demonstrated to the French that they were steadfast and disciplined, and were not to be viewed with contempt (discipline was certainly helped by the absence of alcohol!). These were qualities Graham would later exploit at Barossa and Vitoria.

As will have been seen from the notes on their careers, most of the brigade commanders in Egypt were coming to the end of their time as active soldiers. Moore and Stuart were the exceptions. Below them, though, was a tier of officers who subsequently made good use of their experiences in Egypt. One man who would later enhance his reputation in the Peninsula was Edward Paget, who thought he had taken a mortal wound at the Battle of Alexandria but lived to fight on at Corunna. He led the advance to Oporto, where he lost his arm, before returning to command the 1st Division, falling into French hands during the retreat from Burgos. Baird was also at Corunna, where he lost his arm, which brought his active career to an end. Brent Spencer and Lord Dalhousie commanded divisions under Wellington. William Beresford, colonel of the 88th in Egypt, would rise even higher, finishing up as a field marshal in the Portuguese army.

Richard Fletcher, taken prisoner even before the campaign had properly begun, became Wellington's chief engineer in Portugal and Spain before being killed at San Sebastian. Robert Anstruther demonstrated the same efficiency that had impressed Abercromby, before dying in the final stages of the retreat to Corunna. His position was brilliantly inherited by his friend, George Murray. James McGrigor, surgeon with the 88th but appointed by Baird to head his medical services, went to the Peninsula in 1812 and finally brought efficiency to the medical services there.

This is just a selection of 'Abercromby's pupils'. Others who might be mentioned are Roland (Daddy) Hill, in command of the 90th Foot at Mandorah and Alexandria, who seems to have shared Abercromby's gift of inspiring both love and respect, Lowry Cole, Hely-Hutchinson's military secretary, James Kempt, aide-de-camp first to Abercromby and then Hely-Hutchinson, and John Colborne, at that time just a brevet captain in the 20th Foot. As for Robert Wilson, who served with Hompesch's cavalry and wrote what the historian Piers Mackesy considered the best account of the Egypt campaign, he later founded and commanded the Lusitanian Legion in Portugal. Wellington's only experience of serving under Abercromby was the minor action of Boxtel in 1794, but there were plenty of men serving under him who demonstrated that they had indeed been apt pupils.

As a final thought, it is worth noticing that when in 1847 lists were composed for recipients of the General Service Medal, only just over 1,100 Egypt veterans, of all ranks and all arms of the service, still survived to claim a bar for that campaign. Yet it is significant that something like 50 percent of them had gone on to serve in the Peninsular, where the British army demonstrated beyond all doubt that it could hold its own against Bonaparte's legions.

Appendix I

Uniform

The last complete uniform warrant before the Egypt campaign was published in 1768. Since then, however, there had been many changes, so that in 1801 an amended warrant was issued in an attempt to establish current practice. This resulted in a full description the following year.

General officers wore a red double-breasted, tailed coat, with the tails turned back to show the white lining. The collar was also red but with a dark blue patch to the front. Cuffs and lapels were dark blue. Distinctions of general rank were indicated by the arrangement of gold embroidery. Epaulettes were gold and a crimson sash was worn.

The bicorne hat was worn fore and aft.

Infantry Officers wore a scarlet double-breasted jacket with long tails, which fashion in 1797 dictated was closed to the waist, and laced in the colour and pattern of the regiment. The same colour would also be used for collar, cuffs, and facings. Buttons were a further distinguishing mark. Lapels could be open or partly closed. Field and grenadier officers wore two epaulettes, company officers a single epaulette on the right shoulder, while light company officers had wings. Sashes were tied to the left except in the Highland kilted regiments when they were worn over the left shoulder.

Officers wore white breeches and boots.

Sergeants also wore a scarlet jacket while **other ranks** wore a dull red jacket which quickly faded in the sun. The jacket was closed to the waist, single-breasted and shorter than the officers'. NCOs were distinguished by cord shoulder knots, chevrons not making an appearance until 1802. The sergeant's sash hung to the right.

Officers and men wore the stove-pipe shako, which replaced the cocked hat in in 1800, although some regiments seem to have used the bicorne for officers. Light company men had round hats, which seem to have been copied from the Marines. There is some evidence to suggest these were more widely adopted as the campaign continued. Highland regiments opted for either the highland bonnet or the Tarleton helmet. They also wore knitted hose.

Although breeches, gaiters, and shoes (low boots) were the proscribed nether-wear, Russian duck trousers were advocated by a general order Abercromby issued on Minorca.

Cavalry uniform was established by warrant in 1796. The light cavalry jacket was dark blue, with collar, cuffs and facings in the regimental colour. All the regiments in Egypt had white lace for the men and silver for the officers. Breeches were white, with buff facings. The officers' sash was off-crimson. The 8th Light Dragoons, however, wore light grey jackets and tropical helmets.

The **Royal Artillery** also wore dark blue jackets with red cuffs and collars which were edged in yellow and red. They had yellow tufted shoulder straps, yellow, bastion-pattern lace and white turnbacks. Like the infantry, the regulations required them to wear white breeches and black gaiters, but there is little reason to believe these were retained in Egypt. Until the 1790, gunners wore a high-crowned round hat with a narrow brim. This was subsequently replaced by the bicorne but, again, some units chose to retain the round hat.

The all-officer **Royal Engineers** work dark blue long-tailed coats, with black velvet lapels, cuffs, and a high collar. Their buttons were yellow metal. They wore white breeches and black boots, and the bicorne hat.

Appendix II

Orders of Battle and Unit Strengths

Troops under Abercromby at Minorca, August 1800

1st Brigade	Major General Sir John Craddock	18th, 1/40th, 2/40th, 90th
2nd Brigade	Brigadier General Sir John Doyle	2nd, 8th, 92nd
3rd Brigade	Brigadier General John Stuart	Minorca Regt., De Roll's Regt., Dillon's Regt.
Reserve	Major General John Moore (Brigadier General Hildebrand Oakes was also attached to the Reserve)	28th, 42nd, 50th, 58th, Corsican Rangers, detachment of the 11th Light Dragoons

Troops under Abercromby at Aboukir Bay, March 1801

	Units, with Effective Strengths	Total Strength	Effective Strength
Brigade of Guards Major General Ludlow	1/Coldstream Guards (766), 1/3rd Foot Guards (812)	1,813	1,578
1st Brigade Major General Coote	2/1st (626), 1/54th & 2/54th (974), 92nd (529)	2,535	2,129
2nd Brigade Major General Cradock	8th (439), 13th (561), 18th (411), 90th (727)	2,483	2,135
3rd Brigade Major General Lord Cavan	50th (477), 79th (604)	1,247	1,081
4th Brigade Brigadier General Doyle	2nd (530),* 30th (412), 44th (263), 89th (378)	1,719	1,583
5th Brigade Brigadier General Stuart	Stuart's (Minorca) (929), De Roll's (528), Dillon's (530)	2,113	1,987
Reserve Major General Moore Brigadier General Oakes	23rd (457), 28th (587), 42nd (754), 58th (469), Corsican Rangers (209), 40th (flank companies) (250)	2,954	2,726
Cavalry Brigadier General Finch	11th Lt Dragoons (one troop) (53), 12th Lt Dragoons (474), 26th Lt Dragoons (369), Hompesch's Hussars (138)	1,063	1,034

Artillery Brigadier General Lawson	13th, 14th, 26th, 28th, 55th, 69th, 70th, & 71st companies R.A.	656	627

In addition to the units listed there was a staff corps of 82. Total strength was 14,965, of which 13,222 were infantry.

* The 2nd (Queen's) subsequently transferred to Cavan's brigade to replace the 1/27th and 2/27th which had been left sick at Gibraltar and Malta

Troops under Hely-Hutchinson, Egypt, August 1801

	Units, with Effective Strengths	Total Strength	Effective Strength
Brigade of Guards Major General Earl of Cavan	1/Coldstream (552), 1/3rd Foot Guards (590)	1,804	1,142
1st Brigade Major General Ludlow	25th (526), 1/27th (538), 2/27th (465), 44th (334)	2,389	1,863
2nd Brigade Major General Finch	2/1st (352), 26th (438), 1/54th (381), 2/54th (384)	2,381	1,555
3rd (Foreign) Brigade Brigadier General Stuart	Stuart's (Minorca) (690), De Rolls' (383), Dillon's (393), Watteville's (572)	2,469	2,038
4th Brigade Brigadier General Hope	8th (285), 18th (293), 79th (434), 90th (437)	2,356	1,449
5th Brigade Brigadier General Doyle	30th (269), 50th (337), 89th (311), 92nd (414)	1,935	1,331
6th Brigade Brigadier General Blake	1/20th (604) 2/20th (484), 24th (438), Ancient Irish Fencibles (420)	2,295	1,946
Reserve Major General Moore; Brigadier General Oakes	2nd (327), 23rd (343), 28th (338), 40th (Flank Companies) (146), 42nd (490), 58th (238), Löwenstein's Jägers (397), Chasseurs Britanniques (595), Corsican Rangers (60)	4,565	2,934
Cavalry	11th Lt Dragoons (one troop) (33), 12th Lt Dragoons (398), 26th Lt Dragoons (238), Hompesch's Hussars (109)	1,079	778
Artillery Brigadier General Lawson	13th, 14th, 26th, 28th, 55th, 69th, 70th, & 71st companies R.A.	568	475

Baird's Force at Kosseir and Suez

Royal Artillery	46
Bengal Horse Artillery	134
Bengal Foot Artillery	181
Madras Foot Artillery	253
Bombay Foot Artillery	1
Madras Pioneers	94
8th Light Dragoons	85

10th Foot	954
61st Foot	974
80th Foot	360
86th Foot	355
88th Foot	457
Bengal Volunteers, Native Infantry	631
1st Bombay Regiment, Native Infantry	822
7th Bombay Regiment, Native Infantry	761

As this is a disembarkation return, it is to be inferred that the given strengths are total.

Baird organised a Right Brigade under Colonel Beresford comprising the 10th, 88th, and Bengal Volunteers and a Left Brigade under Lieutenant Colonel Montressor comprising the 61st, 80th, and 1st Bombay Native Infantry. The remaining units were either on detached duty, or reported directly to Baird.

State of the Medical Staff, under the Command of General Sir Ralph Abercromby, K.B., Commander in Chief, etc.

Bay of Aboukir, 2nd March, 1801

Name	Rank	Where doing duty
Thomas Young	Inspector General	H.M.S. Niger.
James Franck	Inspector	Harmony, H.S.
Alex Robertson	Assistant Inspector	Lady Julia Ann, H.S.
Alexr Jameson	Do.	Harmony, H.S.
Willm Fowle	Physician	Rhodes.
Ralph Green	Inspector of F. Hosp	Harmony, H.S.
John Webb	Surgeon	With 79th Regt.
James Pitcairn	Do.	Harmony, H.S.
W. R. Morell	Do.	Lady Julia Ann, H.S.
Ely Crump	Do.	Harmony, H.S.
Alexr Grant	Do.	Harmony, H.S.
J.H. Beaumont	Apothecary	Planter, H.S. Rhodes
Willm Findlay	Do.	Harmony, H.S.
Geo. Dickson	Purveyor	Do.
John Price	Depy Purveyor	Rhodes
Christ. Winnicki	Acting do.	Lady Julia Ann, H.S.
M. Emerson	Do.	Rhodes
Joseph Smith	Hospital Mate	Attached to the Corsican Rangers
-"- Carver	Do	----"---- 1st Bn 54th Regt
Willm Reynolds	Do	----"---- 2nd Bn 54th Regt
Henry West	Do	----"---- 2nd Bn Royals

Name	Rank	Where doing duty
Saml Gissing	Do	Rhodes
Richd Dakin	Do	Do.
James Allen	Do	With the Staff Corps
Willm Brown	Do	Harmony H.S.
-"- Harris	Do	Attached to the 23rd Regt
Thomas Davis	Do	With detachments of 28th & 50th Rts.
Geo. Norman	Do	Harmony, H.S.
Swinton McLeod	Do	Attached to Hompesch's Dragoons.
Saml Steel	Do	Harmony, H.S.
Saml Hare	Do	Lady Julia Ann, H.S.
Douglas Whyte	Do	With the Maltese Pioneers
James Emerson	Purveyor's Clerk	Planter, H.S. Rhodes.
T. Turvey	Do	Harmony, H.S.

N.B. H.S. Signifies Hospital Ship

(Signed)   Thomas Young
Inspector General Army Hospitals

Return of Killed, Wounded, and Missing during the Campaign

	Killed	Wounded	Missing
Officers	22	168	1
Quartermasters		1	1
Sergeants	20	149	2
Drummers	2	17	1
Rank & File	505	2,724	73
Horses	56	20	10

Appendix III

General Orders

Horse Guards, the 16th May, 1801

The recent events which have occurred in Egypt, have induced His Majesty to lay his most gracious commands on His Royal Highness the Commander in Chief, to convey to the troops employed in that country His Majesty's highest approbation of their conduct; at the same time His Majesty has deemed it expedient, that these his gracious sentiments should be communicated to every part of his army, not doubting that all ranks will thereby be inspired with an honourable spirit of emulation, and an eager desire of distinguishing themselves in their country's service.

Under the blessing of Divine Providence, His Majesty ascribes the successes, that have attended the exertions of his troops in Egypt, to that determined bravery, which is inherent in Britons; but His Majesty desires it may be most solemnly and forcibly impressed on the consideration of every part of the army, that it has been a strict observance of order, discipline and military system, which has given it's [sic] full energy to the native valour of the troops, and has enabled them proudly to assert the superiority of the national military character, in situations uncommonly arduous, and under circumstances of peculiar difficulty.

The illustrious example of their commander cannot fail to have made an indelible impression on the gallant troops, at whose head, crowned with victory and glory, he terminated his honourable career; and His Majesty trusts, that a due contemplation of the talents and virtues, which he uniformly displayed in the course of his valuable life, will for ever endear the memory of Sir Ralph Abercromby to the British army.

His Royal Highness the Commander in Chief having thus obeyed His Majesty's commands, cannot forebear to avail himself of the opportunity of recapitulating the leading features of a series of operations so honourable to the British arms.

The boldness of the approach to the coast of Aboukir, in defiance of a powerful and well directed artillery – the orderly formation upon the beach, under the heaviest fire of grape and musquetry – the reception and repulse of the enemy's cavalry and infantry – the subsequent charge of our troops, which decided the victory, and established a footing on the shores of Egypt!

are circumstances of glory never surpassed in the military annals of the world.

The advance of the army, on the 13th March, towards Alexandria, presents the spectacle of a movement of infantry through an open country, who being attacked upon their march, *formed* and *repulsed* the enemy; then advanced in line for three miles, engaged along their whole front, until they drove the enemy to seek his shelter under the protection of his entrenched position. Such had been the order and regularity of the advance.

Upon the 21st March, the united force of the French in Egypt attacked the position of the British army.

An attack, begun an hour before daylight, could derive no advantage over the vigilance of an army ever ready to receive it. The enemy's most vigorous and repeated attacks were directed against the right and the centre. Our infantry fought in the plain, greatly inferiour [sic] in the number of their artillery, and unaided by cavalry.

They relied upon their discipline and courage. The desperate attacks of a veteran cavalry, joined to those of a numerous infantry, which had vainly styled itself Invincible, were every where [sic] repulsed; and a conflict the most severe terminated in one of the most signal victories, which ever adorned the annals of the British nation.

In bringing forward these details, the Commander in Chief does not call upon the army merely to admire, but to emulate such conduct. Every soldier who feels for the honour of his country, while he exults in events so splendid and important in themselves, will henceforth have fresh motives for cherishing and enforcing the practice of discipline; and by uniting in the greatest perfection *order* and *precision* with activity and courage, will seek to uphold, and transmit undiminished to posterity, the glory and honour of the British arms.

Nor is a less useful example to be derived from the conduct of the distinguished Commander, who fell in the field.

His steady observance of discipline – his ever watchful attention to the health and wants of his troops – the persevering and unconquerable spirit, which marked his military career – the splendour of his actions in the field, and the heroism of his death – are worthy the imitation of all who desire, like him, a life of honour and a death of glory.

By order of His Royal Highness the Commander in Chief.
(Signed)   HARRY CALVERT
Colonel and Adjutant General

Appendix IV

Parliamentary Vote of Thanks

On the motion of the Right Honourable Henry Addington, Chancellor of the Exchequer, in the House of Commons, November the 12th, 1801, it is unanimously resolved,

"That the Thanks of this House be given to Lieutenant General Sir John Hely Hutchinson, K.B., for the ability, zeal, and perseverance, so eminently manifested by him in the command of the army serving in Egypt, by which the honour of the British nation had been so signally upheld, and additional lustre reflected on the reputation of the British arms.

"That the Thanks of this House be given to Major General Eyre Coote, second in command; Major Generals John Francis Cradock, the Honourable George James Ludlow, John Moore, Richard Earl of Cavan, David Baird, the Honourable Edward Finch, and to Brigadier Generals John Stewart, the Honourable John Hope, John Doyle, John Blake, Hildebrand Oakes, and Robert Lawson, and the several officers of the army, for their gallant, meritorious, and distinguished services, under the command of Sir John Hely Hutchinson, K.B., by which the honour of the British nation has been so signally upheld, and additional lustre reflected on the reputation of the British arms.

"That the House doth highly approve of and acknowledge the zeal, discipline, and intrepidity uniformly displayed during the arduous and memorable operations of the army in Egypt, by the non-commissioned officers and private soldiers under the command of Lieutenant General Sir John Hely Hutchinson, K.B., and that the same be signified by the commanders of the several corps, who are desired to thank them for their exemplary and gallant behaviour."

On the same day a similar motion was made in the House of Lords, by the Right Honourable Lord Hobart, one of His Majesty's Principal Secretaries of State, and a similar vote of thanks was passed with the same spirit of unanimous approbation.

Bibliography

Archival Sources

Lancashire Infantry Museum, Fulwood Barracks, Preston
    Memoirs of Major Alexander Cosby Jackson.
The National Archives, Kew
    WO17/1757, Office of the Commander in Chief: Monthly Returns to the Adjutant General,
        Egypt 1801.

Primary Sources

Participants in the events between General Abercromby's arrival in Minorca and the surrender of Alexandria are marked with an asterisk

*Anderson, Aeneas, *Journal of the Forces under the Command of Sir Ralph Abercromby in the Mediterranean and Egypt* (London: J.Debrett 1802).
Aspinall, A. (ed), *The Later Correspondence of George III*, Vols II & III (Cambridge: Cambridge University Press, 1963).
Baines, Edward, *History of the Wars of the French Revolution* (London: Longman, 1817).
*Baldwin, George, *Political Recollections Relative to Egypt…with a Narrative of the Ever-Memorable British Campaign in the Spring of 1801* (London: Bulmer, 1802).
Bunbury, Sir Henry, *Narratives of Some Passages of the Great War with France 1799-1810* (London: Peter Davies Ltd, 1927).
* Colborne, John (ed. G. C. Moore Smith), *Colborne: a Singular Talent for War* (Driffield: Leonaur, 2007).
Dundas, David, *Principles of Military Movements Chiefly Applied to Infantry* (London: T.Cadell, 1788).
Fortescue, The Hon. J.W., *Report on the Manuscripts of J.B. Fortescue Esq., preserved at Dropmore* (London: Historical Manuscripts Commission 1905-1908).
Gifford, *History of the Wars Occasioned by the French Revolution from the Commencement of Hostilities in 1792, to the End of the Year 1816* (London: Thomas Kelly, 1817).
*Keith, Admiral (ed. Christopher Lloyd), *The Keith Papers* (London: Naval Record Society 1927).
*Maule, Major Francis, *Memoirs of the Principal Events of the Campaigns of North Holland and Egypt* (London: F.C. & J. Rivington, 1816).
*Miller, Benjamin, 'The Adventures of Serjeant Benjamin Miller whilst serving in the 4th Battalion of the Royal Regiment of Artillery 1796-1815', *Journal of the Society for Army Historical Research*, Vol.7 No.27 (1928), pp.9-51.
*Moiret, Joseph-Marie, (trans. Rosemary Brindle), *Memoirs of Napoleon's Egyptian Expedition 1798-1801* (London: Greenhill Books, 2001).
*Moore, Sir John, (ed. Maurice, J.F.) *The Diary of Sir John Moore* (London: Edward Arnold, 1904).
*Nicol, Daniel, *The Unpublished Diary of Sergeant Daniel Nicol*, in Bruce Low, *With Napoleon at Waterloo* (London: G.Bell & Sons, 1911).
*Robertson, David, *Journal of Sergeant D. Robertson, Late 92nd Foot* (Perth: J. Fisher, 1842).

*Walsh, Thomas, *Journal of the Campaign in Egypt* (London: T.Cadwell & W. Davies, 1803).

*Wilson, R.T., *Narrative of the Expedition to Egypt* (Dublin: W. Corben 1803).

*Wray, Samuel (ed. Gareth Glover), *The Military Adventures of Private Samuel Wray 61st Foot 1796-1815* (Huntingdon: Ken Trotman Publishing, 2009).

Secondary Sources

Alison, Archibald, *History of Europe from the Commencement of the French Revolution to the Restoration of the Bourbons* (London & Edinburgh: Blackwood and Sons, 1847).

Bannatyne, Lt-Col Neil, *History of the Thirtieth Regiment 1689-1881* (Liverpool: Littlebury Bros., 1923).

Bartlett, Keith John, 'The Development of the British Army during the Wars with France 1793-1815' (Unpublished PhD Thesis, Durham University, 1998).

Blanco, Richard L., *Wellington's Surgeon General: Sir James McGrigor* (Durham N.C.: Duke University Press, 1974).

Bruce R., Dickie I., Kiley K., Pavkovic M., Schneid F., *Fighting Techniques of the Napoleonic Age 1792-1815* (London: Amber Books, 2008).

Cantlie, Lt. Gen. Sir Neil, *A History of the Army Medical Department* (London: Longmans Group Ltd, 1973).

Carter, Thomas, *Historical Record of the Forty-Fourth or the East Essex Regiment* (Aldershot: Gale & Polden, 1887).

Cookson, J.E., *The British Armed Nation 1793-1815* (Oxford: Clarendon Press, 1997).

Delavoye, Alex M., *Life of Thomas Graham Lord Lynedoch* (London: Richardson & Co., 1880).

Dodge, Theodore A., *Warfare in the Age of Napoleon* (Boston: Riverside, 1907).

Douglas R.B., *From Valmy to Waterloo: Extracts from the Diary of Captain Charles François* (London: Everett & Co., 1906).

Dunfermline, James Lord, *Lieutenant-General Sir Ralph Abercromby, A Memoir* (Edinburgh: Edmonston & Douglas, 1861).

Fortescue, The Hon. J.W., *A History of the British Army* (London: Macmillan, 1906).

Furber, Holden, *Henry Dundas, First Viscount Melville, 1741-1811* (Oxford: Oxford University Press, 1931).

Gardyne, Lt. Col. C. Greenhill, *The Life of a Regiment: The History of the Gordon Highlanders from its Formation in 1794 to 1816* (Edinburgh: D. Douglas, 1901).

Glover, Richard, *Peninsular Preparation: the Reform of the British Army 1795-1809* (Cambridge: Cambridge University Press, 1970).

Gould, Robert W., *Mercenaries of the Napoleonic Wars* (Brighton: Tom Donovan, 1995).

Grant, Charles, *Napoleon's Campaign in Egypt: Vol.2 – The British Army & Allies* (Leigh-on-Sea: Partizan Press 2007).

Graves, Donald E., *Fix Bayonets: A Royal Welch Fusilier at War 1796-1815* (Staplehurst: Spellmount, 2007).

Guy, Alan J. (ed.), *The Road to Waterloo* (London: National Army Museum 1990).

Hague, William, *William Pitt the Younger* (London: Harper Collins 2004).

Harding-Edgar, John, *Next to Wellington: General Sir George Murray* (Warwick: Helion, 2018).

Harvey, Robert, *The War of Wars: the Epic Struggle between Britain and France 1793-1815* (London: Constable & Robinson Ltd, 2006).

Hill, Joanna, *Wellington's Right Hand Man: Rowland, Viscount Hill* (Stroud: The History Press, 2011).

Holland Rose, J., *William Pitt and the Great War* (London: G. Bell & Sons, 1912).

Knight, Roger, *Britain against Napoleon: the Organization of Victory 1793-1815* (London: Penguin Books, 2014).

Mackesy, Piers, *War without Victory: the Downfall of Pitt 1799-1802* (Oxford: Clarendon Press, 1984).

Mackesy, Piers, *British Victory in Egypt: the End of Napoleon's Conquest* (Abingdon: Routledge, 1995).

Martin, Yves, *The French Army of the Orient 1798-1801: Napoleon's Beloved 'Egyptians'* (Solihull: Helion & Company, 2017).

Matheson, C., *The Life of Henry Dundas, 1st Viscount Melville* (London: Constable & Co., 1933).

Rodger, A.B., *The War of the Second Coalition 1798-1801: a Strategic Commentary* (Oxford: Clarendon Press 1964).

Rothenburg, Gunther E., *The Art of Warfare in the Age of Napoleon* (London: Batsford 1978).

Shankland, Peter, *Beware of Heroes: Admiral Sir Sidney Smith's War against Napoleon* (London: William Kimber, 1975).

Stathern, Paul, *Napoleon in Egypt: 'The Greatest Glory'* (London: Jonathan Cape, 2007).

Ward, Sir A.W. & Gooch, G.P. (eds), *The Cambridge History of British Foreign Policy 1783-1919* (Cambridge: Cambridge University Press, 1922).